A Book of Lives

EDWIN MORGAN was born in Glasgow in 1920. He became lecturer in English at the University of Glasgow, from which he retired as Professor in 1980. He was appointed Poet Laureate of Glasgow in 1999, and received the Queen's Gold Medal for Poetry in 2000. In June 2001 he received the Weidenfeld Prize for Translation for *Phaedra*. In 2004 Edwin Morgan was appointed Scotland's Makar, or Poet Laureate.

D0891130

EDWIN MORGAN

A Book of Lives

CARCANET

First published in Great Britain in 2007 by
Carcanet Press Limited
Alliance House
Cross Street
Manchester M2 7AQ

Copyright © Edwin Morgan 2007

A CIP catalogue record for this book is available from the British Library

ISBN 978 1 85754 918 8

The publisher acknowledges financial assistance from Arts Council England

Typeset by XL Publishing Services, Tiverton
Printed and bound in England by SRP Ltd, Exeter

Contents

Acknowledgements

Thanks are due to the editors of the following publications in which poems first appeared: *Addicted to Brightness* (Long Lunch Press), *The Book of Questions, The Hand that Sees: poems for the quincentenary of the Royal College of Surgeons of Edinburgh* (RCOSOE and SPL), the *Herald*, the *London Review of Books, Map, New Writing 13, Nova Scotia: New Scottish Speculative Fiction* (Crescent), *Painted, Spoken, PN Review, Proof, Scotland on Sunday*, the *Scotsman, The Wallace Muse* (Luath).

'For the Opening of the Scottish Parliament' was commissioned by the Parliament and read at the opening ceremony on 9 October 2004. Scottish Parliamentary copyright, reprinted by permission.

'Acknowledge the Unacknowledged Legislators!' was written for the launch of the Cross-Party Group on Scottish Writing and Publishing 2005.

The Battle of Bannockburn was published with Robert Baston's Latin text in 2004 jointly by Akros Publications, Mariscat Press and the Scottish Poetry Library.

'Retrieving & Renewing' was commissioned by the Association for Scottish Literary Studies.

'Valentine Weather' was published online by the Scottish Poetry Library.

'Three Songs' was written for the band Idlewild.

'My First Octopus' was written to be broadcast by BBC radio on National Poetry Day 2004.

Gorgo and Beau was commissioned by BBC Radio Scotland and broadcast on 29 December 2003.

'The Welcome' was written for the International Federation of Library Authorities (IFLA) Conference 2002.

'Brothers and Keepers' was written for a conference of social workers.

Love and a Life was published by Mariscat Press in 2003.

For the Opening of the Scottish Parliament, 9 October 2004

Open the doors! Light of the day, shine in; light of the mind, shine out!
We have a building which is more than a building.
There is a commerce between inner and outer, between brightness and
shadow, between the world and those who think about the world.
Is it not a mystery? The parts cohere, they come together like petals of a
flower, yet they also send their tongues outward to feel and taste the
teeming earth.
Did you want classic columns and predictable pediments? A growl of old
Gothic grandeur? A blissfully boring box?
Not here, no thanks! No icon, no IKEA, no iceberg, but curves and
caverns, nooks and niches, huddles and heavens, syncopations and
surprises. Leave symmetry to the cemetery.
But bring together slate and stainless steel, black granite and grey granite,
seasoned oak and sycamore, concrete blond and smooth as silk – the
mix is almost alive – it breathes and beckons – imperial marble it is
not!

Come down the Mile, into the heart of the city, past the kirk of St Giles
and the closes and wynds of the noted ghosts of history who drank
their claret and fell down the steep tenement stairs into the arms of
link-boys but who wrote and talked the starry Enlightenment of
their days –
And before them the auld makars who tickled a Scottish king's ear with
melody and ribaldry and frank advice –
And when you are there, down there, in the midst of things, not set upon
an hill with your nose in the air,
This is where you know your parliament should be
And this is where it is, just here.

What do the people want of the place? They want it to be filled with
thinking persons as open and adventurous as its architecture.
A nest of fearties is what they do not want.
A symposium of procrastinators is what they do not want.
A phalanx of forelock-tuggers is what they do not want.
And perhaps above all the droopy mantra of 'it wizny me' is what they do
not want.
Dear friends, dear lawgivers, dear parliamentarians, you are picking up a
thread of pride and self-esteem that has been almost but not quite,
oh no not quite, not ever broken or forgotten.

When you convene you will be reconvening, with a sense of not wholly the
power, not yet wholly the power, but a good sense of what was once
in the honour of your grasp.
All right. Forget, or don't forget, the past. Trumpets and robes are fine,
but in the present and the future you will need something more.
What is it? We, the people, cannot tell you yet, but you will know about it
when we do tell you.
We give you our consent to govern, don't pocket it and ride away.
We give you our deepest dearest wish to govern well, don't say we have no
mandate to be so bold.
We give you this great building, don't let your work and hope be other
than great when you enter and begin.
So now begin. Open the doors and begin.

Acknowledge the Unacknowledged Legislators!

Go on, squawk at the font, you chubby Scotty.
You have a long song ahead of you, do you know that?
Of course not, but you let the ghost of a chuckle
Emerge and flicker as if you had thrown
Your very first chuckle and the water was playful.
It will be, and gurly too, and full of dread
Once you are grown and reckoning ahead.

So squeal a little, kick a little, what's a few drops
On that truly enormous human brow.
Man is *chelovek*, the Russians say,
The one with a forehead, the one with forethought,
The one whose mumbling and chuntering will not do,
Who knows it will not do, who lolls or bounces
Half-formed but strains for form, to be a child
And not a bundle! The bungler, the mumbler
Takes the deepest breath we are allowed,
Whistles the horizon's dawn right down
Across the book of earth, audits the figures,
Tongue and teeth and lips in line, near-perfect,
Ye see yon birkie ca'd a lord, the poet
Has hooked one leg over his simple chair-arm,
Sometimes tapping the beat upon his snuff-box,
Sometimes singing an old and well-loved air
To startlingly original effect.
He'll print it too! Won't it be in a book?
An open mind is proper in this case.
It's only poetry, after all. Someone –
I can't remember thousands of scribbling names –
Has said 'Poetry makes nothing happen.'
I find that slightly fundamentalist.
Yes, but do I go along with it?
I do not go along with it. No, I don't.
Do I protest too much? Probably!

Think of what I said about the child.
He is a man now, let us talk to him.
Ask him how far he thinks his *birkie*
Registers on a Richter scale of insult.
He's dead? Well, get a good dictionary.

Talk's the thing. Dialogue's the thing.
If any parliamentarian should be so remiss
As to think writers are interchangeable,
Or stupid, or irrelevant, or poor doomy creatures,
Punishments may have to be devised,
I say *may*, we want to persuade, not scold.
What is it but language that clamps
A country to glory? Ikons, concertos,
Pietàs, gamelans, gondolas, didgeridoos,
Luboks, a brace of well-tuned sleigh-bells –
These are very fine, of course they are.
But better still, always far better still
Is the sparkling articulacy of the word,
The scrubbed round table where poet and legislator
Are plugged in to the future of the race,
Guardians of whatever is the case.

The Cost of Pearls

Do you want to challenge that dervish Scotland?
Even and only being interrogated
by a swash of centenarian mussels
black-encrusted and crusty with it?
When they folded their arms and gave such a click
it could be heard right down Strathspey,
did you reckon the risk of a dialogue was minimal?
'Come on then, have at you!' It was like an old play
though far from funny. 'All that winking stuff,
that metal, those blades,
you think we don't know death when we smell it?'
'Your nose deceives you. We are observers, explorers.
We heard there was a murmuring of mussels,
a clatter and a chatter
somewhere in the gravel-beds of unbonny Scotland,
almost like voices threatening something – '
'Damn sure we were threatening something! Do you know
a thousand of us were killed in one day
not long ago – ' 'I heard it was eight hundred – '
'Eight hundred, ten hundred, it was a massacre.
Your pearl poachers breenged through our domains like demons
with their great gully knives and scythed us to shreds
for what might be, most likely might not be,
a pearl, a pearl of price, a jeweller's price.

I hear a shuffling of papers. Prepare yourself.
We are our wisest, neither clique nor claque
but full conclave. We want to know,
and we will know, what is it gives you
your mania for killing. Don't interrupt!
For a few smouldering prettinesses
at neck and brow you would ransack
a species. I said don't interrupt,
we have all the time in the world
and I can hear the steady footfall
(that's a joke, you may smile)
as our oldest and wisest, worthily High Mussel
at a hundred and forty-nine, filtering and harrumphing
(no, you must not smile now),
angrily kicking the gravel, and with a last sift and puff
(no no, this is not funny, think of his powers)
commands the interrogation to begin.'

Lines for Wallace

Is it not better to forget?
It is better not to forget.
Betrayal not to be forgotten,
Vindictiveness not to be forgotten,
Triumphalism not to be forgotten.
Body parts displayed
At different points of the compass,
Between hanging and hacking
The worst, the disembowelling.
Blood raised in him, fervent
Blood raced in him, fervent
Blood razed in him, for ever
Fervent in its death.
For Burns was right to see
It was not only on the field
That Scots would follow this man
With blades and war-horn
Sharp and shrill
But with brains and books
Where the idea of liberty
Is impregnated and impregnates.
Oh that too is sharp and shrill
And some cannot stand it
And some would not allow it
And some would rather die
For the regulated music
Of Zamyatin's Polyhymnia
Where nothing can go wrong.
Cinema sophisticates
Fizzed with disgust at the crudities
Braveheart held out to them.
Over the cheeks of some
(Were they less sophisticated?)
A tear slipped unbidden.
Oh yes it did. I saw it.
The power of Wallace
Cuts through art
But art calls attention to it
Badly or well.
In your room, in the street,

Even my god if it came to it
On a battlefield,
Think about it,
Remember him.

The Battle of Bannockburn

A Translation of 'Metrum de Praelio Apud Bannockburn', by Robert Baston

Pain is my refrain, pain comes dragging its rough train.
Laughter I disdain, or my elegy would be in vain.
The Ruler of All, who can cause tears to stall,
Is the true witness to call if you want any good to befall
Those under thrall, roped-up in filthy unsilky pall.
I weep for all that fall in that iron funeral.
I raise my battle-lament, sitting here in my tent.
And the blame for this event? God knows to whom it is sent!

This is a double realm: each itches to dominate:
Neither hands over the helm for the other to subjugate.
England and Scotland – which one is the Pharisee?
Each has to stand guard, and not fall into the sea!
Hence those pumped-up factions dyed with crimson blood,
Squads in battle-actions slaughtered crying in the mud,
Hence this waste of men, crossed out by war's black pen,
Whole peoples sunk in the fen, still fighting, again and again,
Hence white faces in the ground, hence white faces of the drowned,
Hence huge grief is found, cries with which the stars are crowned,
Hence wars that devastate field and farm and state.
How can I relate each massacre that lies in wait?

It is June Thirteen Fourteen, and here I set the scene,
The Baptist's head on a tureen, the battle on Stirling green.
Oh I am not glued to ancient schism and feud,
But my weeping is renewed for the dead I saw and rued.
Who will lend me the water I need to baptise these forays?
Already torrents and springs overwhelm my heart-strings
And break the rings of my singing of better things.

The governor of the land has that land's domination,
At his slightest command a great force is in full formation.
Huzzas from English throats; Scots in eager armour;
Soldiers with high notes may not live up to their clamour!
See how the English king, consulting and considering,
Asks boldest men to bring fear to the Scots, penetrating
Chivalry with chivalry, country into country!

Charging the nobility to draw on every ability,
What a brilliant band of magnates mustering and swerving!
They want you bowing and serving! Scotland, take sword in hand!

Infantry scenting battle crisscross county and shire.
Sailors all afire plough seas till the halyards rattle.
Armour-bearer and squire hasten with bridles and reins.
Cavalry seethes and clanks, trumpeters strain their veins.
All the belligerent ranks surge forward bloodthirsty and fierce
(Dark death will pierce, if it wishes, those high-fives and swanks!).
A knight mounts his horse, he is braced and bright for the fight,
His face breathes force, his rich garb woos the sight.
Four Germans arrive, offer free services:
Will the English derive help from these pseudo-mercenaries?
All I know is that arms are handed out to all;
No one says no if the man seems handy and tall;
Safe hands for a shield, for a lance, for a bloody field,
Strong not to yield, skilled, war-welcoming, steeled.

They spent the night drinking, bragging how they'd bring down the Scots.
Their boasts were unthinking, they mouthed windy thoughts.
They drowsed, they snored, they were superhuman, they ignored
Fate, they soared in their dreams right overboard.
What would they do when their banners fluttered in the sun?
They were about to be run through, all arrogance undone!

The herald blares his horn, the baleful battle-news is born.
Gall from honey is torn by the fingers of such a storm.
Now Scots men-at-arms mustered by war's alarms
Have no magic charms but boldness and brash brawny arms.
Hey, Saxon standard-bearer, terrify the Scots with that flag!
Your troops are action-famished there, they won't linger or lag.
Archer, stretch your bow and stretch your bow.
Let arrows fetch devastation from that side to the foe.
Spearmen, flash lightning from this side. Breathe deep, let go.
Make it a smash, a crash, let death let them know!
Slingshot-boy, spread panic with your stones,
It is no toy, fill ditches with the dead and with dying groans!
All must stand fast; crossbows are drawn at last;
The swarm is cast, bolts batter and buzz and blast.
Spears are at hand, the Saxon satraps look grand,
But things are at a stand, clear strategy seems banned.

The Scottish king forms, and informs his potent throng,
Infantry and cavalry. Oh what an array, so ordered and strong!
The king's voice is heard, inspiring the nobility,
Giving the measured but fiery word to the men of quality.
He checks and directs the formation of his eager troops.
Others are worthless, he reckons, and their star droops.
He incites and delights the multitude of his men.
He flytes and derides the English – their treaties not worth a hen.
He said, and he led; all fingers must be firm to the end.
Never swerve from a serf of the shameless Saxon blend!
The masses are sassy, they relish the royal rousing.
They will stand like a band and give the Saxons a sousing!

Unity is strength, says the king; each knows what each must do.
Here at length is the war; here, the weapons that are due.
A jet of arrows will get a bloody groin or two!
And let a flurry of snake-biting spears bring death to not a few!
Let each sleek spear leave the leaders without cheer,
When soon it must appear that death and defeat are near!
Let the axeman slice limb from trunk with professional flair,
Let his action be a brandishing of something immovably there!
A sword-point cannot hide; no one, on no side, sees no readiness.
Only fate knows those who replace the dead in lucky steadiness

Wicked hands have invented a trap for trampling horses:
Ditches with stakes, planted to stop them in their courses.
The plebs have kindly dug and dug to spatchcock the cavalry
But those on foot too have the rug pulled out from their revelry,
Not one of those men will clamber on horseback again.
Thus lords, though in pain, will be lorded over, complaining in vain.

The invading army is summoned, the Scottish army is numbered.
The frontline phalanx is ordered, the king's bodyguard is sworded.
The leaders of both sides decide to send out scouts,
Who come back to divide good counsel with deadly doubts.
Bloody Sunday opens with the rumbling of omens
For the Sassenach yeomen, moment by moment.
The first assaults come whirling on the dry ground of Stirling.
The English host shines splendid, but soon the glitter is ended.

Pain is great, pain is piled upon pain.
Rage is in spate, rage rages as rain.
Clamour is not blate, a frontline-to-frontline refrain.

Bravery – checkmate, brave follows brave in vain.
Ardour cannot wait, ardour is furious and fain.
Fighters blame fate, fortitude is on the wane.
Amazement is the state, amazement spreads its stain.
It is a fuzzy slate, order is slated and slain.
Uproar cannot abate, Abel loses to Cain.

Black Monday gives a new life to the deadly plague.
Scots blow the plague by lucky force upon the English flag.
The Angles are like angels glittering high and proud,
But valorous and vassal both are labouring under a cloud.
English eyes scan the skies for Scots ambushes to arise,
But Scots are near, are here, full size, surprise surprise!
The plebs are roaring and swearing, but when things get scary
They wilt and are weary, they crack under the fury.
The ogre is mediocre, the Scots are stockier.
Who will be known as victor? The Dutiful Doctor.
A reckless raid pretends to be robustly arrayed.
Deep sobs escalade from the face's palisade,
Scots find a route to rush fast forward on foot,
Brandishing boot on boot, fielding loot for loot.
What snatching and catching, what bruising and broostling, what grief!
What warhorns and warnings, what winding and wirrying, no relief!
What slashing and slaughtering, what wounding and wailing, what a rout!
What lurking and lunging, what grabbing and groaning, what a turnabout!
What roaring and rearing, what shrinking and shaking, what lassooing!
What cloaking and collecting, what snipping and specking, what undoing!
Bellies will be empty. Both broadswords and bodies are booty.
So many fatherless children to clutch at futurity!

Clare of Gloucester, fosterer of courage, earl and landlord,
Ah, you are out among the dead, by God's avenging word.
Lionlike Clifford, you have stiffened at the sword's point,
So many blows from the enemy have jarred you at every joint.
William Marshal, macho, martial in the battle-line,
Scottish hardmen hacked you down with dastardly design.
Edmund Mauley, bold and manly royal steward,
Hosts of hostility have got you scotched and skewered.
Tiptoft, top fighter, like a blazing fire
Your grave is blades and staves, and the banners retire.
Noble Argentan, great gentleman, sweet Giles,
I would fain have fainted when I saw you in those falling files.

What is truth worth? How can I sing about so much blood?
Could even tragedy bare its breast to show such cut and thud?
The names may be famous but I do not know them all.
I cannot number the humblings and tumblings of hundreds that fall.
Many are mown down, many are thrown down,
Many are drowned, many are found and bound.
Many are taken in chains for a stated ransom.
So some are rising, riding rich high and handsome
Who before the war were poor and threadbare souls.
The battlefield is barren but piled with spoils.
Shouts and taunts and vengeful cuts and brawls –
I saw, but what can I say? A harvest I did not sow!
Guile is not my style. Justice and peace are what I would show.
Anyone who has more in store, let him write the score.
My mind is numb, my voice half–dumb, my art a blur.

I am a Carmelite, and my surname is Baston.
I grieve that I survive a happening so harrowing and ghastly.
If it is my sin to have left out what should be in,
Let others begin to record it, without rumour or spin.

James IV To his Treasurer

Oh for Christ's sake gie the signor his siller.
Alchemist my erse, but he's hermless, is he no?
He'll never blaw us up in oor beds, I tak it.
If makkin wings is his new-fanglt ploy
It'll no cost the earth – a wheen o skins,
Or silk if he can get it, wid for the struts,
Fedders, is he intae fedders?, gum, oh aye,
Ane prentice or twa, keep their mooths shut,
It micht be kinrik secret stuff, ye ken,
Fleg the enemy, sky black wi baukie-birds,
My Gode, whit could ye no drap on thaim –
This signor, whit's he cried, Damiano,
Tell him he'll get his purse, but tell him:
Nae mair elixirs, quintessences, *faux* gowd!

Ye say he wants tae loup frae the castle-waws
At Stirling. Weel weel, that's a dandy step,
And lat the warld tak tent o sic a ferlie.
But jist suppose there's a doonbeat scenario
For Signor Damiario: ane wing snapt aff,
He faws, he breks a leg, it's a richt scunner.
Signor, help is at haun! Ane speedy litter
Wheechs him tae Edinburgh, whaur the new College
O Surgeons welcomes him with aipen erms.
I'll be there, signor, a king can set a leg.
I need mair practice, but I can dae it, oh yes.
And noo for the warst-case scenario:
The bird-man whuds doon splat, doon tae his daith.
Oh what a bonus: we'll hae ane public dissection.
My Charter will hae wings, it'll tak aff,
Whit can we no dae gif we set oor minds tae it?
Tell Signor Damiano, be he limpin or be he a corp,
The College o Surgeons stauns honed and skeely and eident.

Retrieving & Renewing

Forget your literature? – forget your soul.
If you want to see your country hale and whole
Turn back the pages of fourteen hundred years.
Surely not? Oh yes, did you expect woad and spears?
In *Altus Prosator* the bristly blustery land
Bursts in buzz and fouth within a grand
Music of metrical thought. Breathes there the man
With soul so dead –? Probably! But a scan
Would show his fault was ignorance:
Don't follow him. Cosmic circumstance
Hides in nearest, most ordinary things.
Find Scotland – find inalienable springs.

Planet Wave

The first half of this sequence of poems, commissioned by the Cheltenham International Jazz Festival, and set to music by Tommy Smith, was first performed in the Cheltenham Town Hall on 4 April 1997.

In the Beginning
(20 Billion BC)

Don't ask me and don't tell me. I was there.
It was a bang and it was big. I don't know
what went before, I came out with it.
Think about that if you want my credentials.
Think about that, me, it, imagine it
as I recall it now, swinging in my spacetime hammock,
nibbling a moon or two, watching you.
What am I? You don't know. It doesn't matter.
I am the witness, I am not in the dock.
I love matter and I love anti-matter.
Listen to me, listen to my patter.

Oh what a day (if it was day) that was!
It was as if a fist had been holding fast
one dense packed particle too hot to keep
and the fingers had suddenly sprung open
and the burning coal, the radiant mechanism
had burst and scattered the seeds of everything,
out through what was now space, out
into the pulse of time, out, my masters,
out, my friends, so, like a darting shoal,
like a lion's roar, like greyhounds released,
like blown dandelions, like Pandora's box,
like a shaken cornucopia, like an ejaculation –

I was amazed at the beauty of it all,
those slowly cooling rosy clouds of gas,
wave upon wave of hydrogen and helium,
spirals and rings and knots of fire, silhouettes
of dust in towers, thunderheads, tornadoes;
and then the stars, and the blue glow of starlight
lapislazuliing the dust-grains –

I laughed, rolled like a ball, flew like a dragon,
zigzagged and dodged the clatter of meteorites
as they clumped and clashed and clustered into
worlds, into this best clutch of nine
whirled in the Corrievreckan of the Sun.
The universe had only just begun.
I'm off, my dears. My story's still to run!

The Early Earth
(3 Billion BC)

Planets, planets – they seem to have settled
into their orbits, round their golden lord,
their father, except he's not their father,
they were all born together, in that majestic wave
of million-degree froth and jet and muck:
who would have prophesied the dancelike separation,
the nine globes, with their moons and rings, rare –
do you know how rare it is, dear listeners,
dear friends, do you know how rare you are?
Don't you want to be thankful? You suffer too much?
I'll give you suffering, but first comes thanks.

Think of that early wild rough world of earth:
lurid, restless, cracking, groaning, heaving,
swishing through space garbage and flak,
cratered with a thousand dry splashdowns
painted over in molten granite. Think of hell,
a mineral hell of fire and smoke. You're there.
What's it all for? Is this the lucky planet?
Can you down a pint of lava, make love
to the Grand Canyon, tuck a thunderbolt
in its cradle? Yes and no, folks, yes and no.
You must have patience with the story.

I took myself to the crest of a ridge
once it was pushed up and cooled.
There were more cloudscapes than earthquakes.
You could walk on rock and feel rain.
You shivered but smiled in the fine tang.

Then I came down to stand in the shallows
of a great ocean, my collar up to the wind,
but listen, it was more than the wind I heard,
it was life at last, emerging from the sea,
shuffling, sliding, sucking, scuttling, so small
that on hands and knees I had to strain my eyes.
A trail of half-transparent twitchings!
A scum of algae! A greening! A breathing!
And no one would stop them, volcanoes wouldn't stop them!
How far would they go? What would they not try?
I punched the sky, my friends, I punched the sky.

End of the Dinosaurs
(65 Million BC)

If you want life, this is something like it.
I made myself a tree-house, and from there
I could see distant scrubby savannas
but mostly it was jungle, lush to bursting
with ferns, palms, creepers, reeds, and the first flowers.
Somewhere a half-seen slither of giant snakes,
a steamy swamp, a crocodile-drift
in and out of sunlight. But all this, I must tell you,
was only background for the rulers of life,
the dinosaurs. Who could stand against them?
They pounded the earth, they lazed in lakes,
they razored through the sultry air.

                              Hear,
if you will, the scrunchings of frond and branch
but also of joint and gristle. It's not a game.
I watched a tyrannosaurus rise on its hindlegs
to slice a browsing diplodocus, just like that,
a hiss, a squirm, a shake, a supper –
velociraptors scattered like rabbits.

It didn't last. It couldn't? I don't know.
Were they too big, too monstrous, yet wonderful
with all the wonder of terror. Were there other plans?
I saw the very day the asteroid struck:
mass panic, mass destruction, mass smoke and mass ash
that broke like a black wave over land and sea,

billowing, thickening, choking, until no sun
could pierce the pall and no plants grew and no
lizards however terrible found food and no
thundering of armoured living tons disturbed
the forest floor and there was no dawn roar,
only the moans, only the dying groans
of those bewildered clinker-throated ex-time-lords,
only, at the end, skulls and ribs and hatchless
eggs in swamps and deserts
left for the inheritors –
my friends, that's you and me
branched on a different tree:
what shall we do, or be?

In the Cave
(30,000 BC)

Dark was the cave where I discovered man,
but he made it, in his own way, bright.
The cavern itself was like a vast hall
within a labyrinth of tunnels. Children
set lamps on ledges. Women fanned a hearth.
Suddenly with a jagged flare of torches
men trooped in from the hunt, threw down
jagged masses of meat, peeled off furs
by the fire till they were half-naked, glistening
with sweat, stocky intelligent ruffians,
brought the cave alive with rapid jagged speech.
You expected a grunt or two? Not so.
And music, surely not? You never heard
such music, I assure you, as the logs crackled
and the meat sizzled, when some with horns and drums
placed echoes in the honeycomb of corridors.
This was no roaring of dinosaurs.

I joined them for their meal. They had a bard,
a storyteller. Just like me, I said.
I told him about distant times. He interrupted.
'I don't think I believe that. Are you a shaman?
If so, where's your reindeer coat? Have another drink.
If you're a shape-shifter, I'm a truth-teller.
Drink up, we call it beer, it's strong, it's good.

You should've been out with us today,
it isn't every day you catch a mammoth,
keep us fed for a week, fur too, tusks –
nothing wasted. Spears and arrows both,
that's what you need, plus a good crowd a boys,
goo' crowda boys. Take s'more beer, go on.
See mamm'ths? Mamm'ths're fuck'n stupit.
Once they're down they can't get up. Fuck em.
Y'know this, y'know this, ole shaman-man,
we'll be here long after mamm'ths're gone.'

He stumbled to his feet, seized a huge torch and ran
along the wall, making such a wave of sparks
the painted mammoths kicked and keeled once more.

A deep horn gave that movie flicker its score.

The Great Flood
(10,000 BC)

Rain, rain, and rain again, and still more rain,
rain and lightning, rain and mist, a month of downpours,
till the earth quaked gruffly somewhere and sent
tidal waves over the Middle Sea,
tidal waves over the Middle East,
tidal wave and rain and tidal wave
to rave and rove over road and river and grove.
I skimmed the water-level as it rose:
invisible the delta! gone the headman's hut!
drowned at last even the stony jebel!

I groaned at whole families swept out to sea.
Strong horses swam and swam but sank at last.
Little treasures, toys, amulets were licked
off pitiful ramshackle village walls.
Weapons, with the hands that held them, vanished.

So what to do? Oh never underestimate
those feeble scrabbling panting gill-less beings!
Hammers night and day on the high plateau!
Bitumen smoking! Foremen swearing! A boat,
an enormous boat, a ship, a seafarer,

caulked, battened, be-sailed, oar-banked, crammed
with life, human, animal, comestible,
holy with hope, bobbing above the tree-tops,
set off to shouts and songs into the unknown
through rags and carcases and cold storks' nests.

The waters did go down. A whaleback mountain
shouldered up in a brief gleam of sludge,
nudged the ark and grounded it. Hatches gaped.
Heads smelt the air. Some bird was chirping.
And then a rainbow: I laughed, it was too much.
But as they tottered out with their bundles,
their baskets of tools, their goats, their babies,
and broke like a wave over the boulders and mosses,
I thought it was a better wave than the wet one
that had almost buried them all.

Water
we came from, to water we may return.
But keep webbed feet at arm's length! Build!
That's what I told them: rebuild, but build!

The Great Pyramid
(2,500 BC)

A building of two million blocks of stone
brought from beyond the Nile by barge and sledge,
dragged up on ramps, trimmed and faced smooth
with bronze chisels and sandstone pads, what a gleam,
what a dazzle of a tomb, what mathematics
in that luminous limestone point against the blue,
the blue above and the yellow below,
the black above and the silver below,
the stars like sand-grains, the pyramid joining them –
You should have seen it, my friends, I must confess
it made a statement to me, and you can scrub
conventional wisdom about the megalomania
of mummies awaiting the lift-off to eternity.
The architects, the surveyors, the purveyors,
the laundresses and cooks, and the brawny gangs
who were not slaves, they would go on strike
if some vizier was stingy with grain or beer:

it was the first mass effort to say
We're here, we did this, this is not nature
but geometry, see it from the moon some day!

Oh but the inauguration, the festivity, the holiday –
I joined the throng, dear people, how could I not?
The sun gave its old blessing, gold and hot and high.
The procession almost rose to meet it:
what was not white linen was lapis lazuli,
what was not lapis lazuli was gold,
there was a shining, a stiff rustling, a solemnity,
the pharaoh and his consort carried in golden chairs,
the bodyguards were like bronze statues walking,
there were real desert men with hawks, severe
as hawks themselves, there were scribes and singers,
black dancing-girls oiled to black gold – wild –
and then the long powerful snake of the workers
which rippled from the Nile to the four great faces
and coiled about them for the dedication.

And the bursting wave of music, the brilliant discords,
the blare, the triumph, the steps of the sound-lords
bore away like a storm my storyteller's words.

On the Volga
(922 AD)

I fancied a change, bit of chill, nip in the air,
went up into Russia, jogged along the Volga,
quite brisk, breath like steam, blood on the go,
ready for anything, you know the feeling.
But I was not as ready as I thought.

I came upon a camp of Vikings, traders
bound south for the Black Sea, big men, fair,
tattooed, their ships at anchor in the river.
Their chief had died, I was to witness
the ritual of cremation. It is so clear –
dear people, I must speak and you must hear –

A boat was dragged on shore, faggots were stacked,
they dressed the dead man in cloth of gold, laid him

in a tent on deck. Who would die with him?
A girl volunteered – yes, a true volunteer –
walked about singing, not downcast, stood
sometimes laughing, believe me, talking to friends.
What did she think of the dog that was cut in two,
thrown into the ship? Nothing, it was what was done.
The horses? The chief must have his beasts
by his side on that black journey. She,
when her time had come, went into six tents
one by one, and lay with the men there.
Each entered her gently, saying 'Tell your master
I did this only for love of you.' Strong drink
was given her, cup after cup. Stumbling, singing,
she was lifted onto the ship, laid down, held,
stabbed by a grim crone and strangled simultaneously
by two strong men, so no one could say who killed her.
Shields were beaten with staves to drown her cries.

Sex and death, drink and fire – the fourth was to come.
The ship was torched, caught quickly, spat, crackled,
burned, birchwood, tent-cloth, flesh, cloth of gold
melted in the blaze that was fanned even faster
by a storm blowing up from the west, sending
wave after wave of smoke in flight across the river.

My friends, do you want to know what you should feel?
I can't tell you, but feel you must. My story's real.

The Mongols
(1200–1300 AD)

The Pope sent a letter to the Great Khan, saying
'We do not understand you. Why do you not obey?
We are under the direct command of Heaven.'
The Great Khan replied to the Pope, saying
'We do not understand you. Why do you not obey?
We are under the direct command of Heaven.'
I must admit I turned a couple of cartwheels
when I found these letters. Mongol chutzpah,
I thought, something new in the world, black comedy
you never get from the solemn Saracens.
Why not? Heaven has given them the earth

from Lithuania to Korea, they ride
like the wind over a carpet of bones.
They have laws, they record, they study the stars.
They are a wonder, but what are they for?

I stood in waves of grass, somewhere in Asia
(that's a safe address), chewing dried lamb
and scanning the low thundery sky,
when a column of Mongol soldiers came past,
halted, re-formed, were commended by their shaman
to the sky-god Tengri who was bending the blue
in order to bless them. Instruments appeared
as if from nowhere, a band, war music
but very strange, stopped as suddenly,
except for the beat of kettledrums as the troop
moved forward. Were they refreshed, inspired?
Who knows? But oh that measured conical bob
of steel caps, gleam of lacquered leather jerkins,
indefatigable silent wolf-lope!
Were they off to make rubble of some great city?
I think they were off to enlarge the known world.
They trotted out of sight; the horsemen followed;
a cold wind followed that, with arrows of rain.
Even in my felt jacket I shivered. Yet –
yet they were there to shake the mighty in their seats.
They were like nature, dragons, volcanoes. Keep awake!
Are you awake, dear people? Are you ready for the Horde,
the page-turner, the asteroid, the virtual sword?

Magellan
(1521 AD)

Cliffs of Patagonia, coldest of coasts,
and the ships sweeping south-west into the strait
which was to be Magellan's: like St Elmo's fire
I played in the rigging, I was tingling, it was good
to see the navigator make determination
his quadrant and his compass into the unknown.
A mutiny? Always hang ringleaders. He did.
One ship wrecked, one deserted? Right. Right.
On with the other three. This channel of reefs,
a wild month needling through, cursing the fogs,

crossing himself as he saw the land of fire,
Tierra del Fuego, flaring its petroleum hell,
then out at last into what seemed endless waves –
Magellan stared at a watery third of the world.
West! West and north! What squalls! What depths!
What sea-monsters I watched from the crow's-nest!
The starving and parching below, the raving, the rats
for dinner, the gnawing of belts! Magellan held
his piercing eye and salt-white beard straight on
to landfall, to the Marianas and the Philippines and
to death. I shuddered at that beach of blood
where he was hacked to pieces. Would you not?

And would you not rejoice that his lieutenant
sailed on, sailed west, sailed limping back,
one tattered ship, sailed home again to Spain
to prove the world was round. And they would need
more ships, for it was mostly water. A ball
with no edge you could fall from – that seemed fine.
But a wet ball in space, what could hold it together?
Every triumph left a trail of questions.
Just as it should, I told the geographers.

Don't you agree, folks, that's the electric prod
to keep us on the move? Don't care for prods,
put your head in a bag, that's what I say.
Well, I'm given to saying things like that,
I'm free.

      Great Ferdinand Magellan,
sleep in peace beneath the seas.
The world's unlocked, and you gave us the keys.

Copernicus
(1543 AD)

In the Baltic there are many waves,
but in Prussian fields I saw, and did not see,
the wave of thought that got the earth to move.
Copernicus's Tower, as they call it,
took its three storeys to a viewing platform,
open, plenty of night, no telescope though.
I used to watch the light go on, then off,
and a dark figure occlude a star
as he would see the moon do. Moon and sun
swung round the earth, unless you were blind.
No. Earth and moon swung round the sun
and earth swung round itself. Mars, Venus,
all, a family, a system, and the system was solar.

Who was he, and does it matter? No stories
are told about this man who kicked the earth
from its false throne. Luther called him a fool
but Luther was the fool. He had servants,
rode a horse, healed the sick, heard cases,
administered a province, but his big big eyes
smouldered like worlds still unadministered.
Big hands too – but he never married.
War swirled round his enclave, peasants starved,
colleagues fled, he stayed in the smoking town –
something of iron there. A play lampooned him
but nothing could stop this patient revolutionary.
I heard them knock at the door of his death-chamber
to bring him the book of his life's labours
but I doubt if he saw it – he gave no sign –
that tremendous title *On the Revolutions*
(and what a pun that was) *of the Heavenly Spheres*
floated above the crumpled haemorrhage and sang
like an angel, a human angel cast loose at last
to voyage in a universe that would no more stand still
than the clouds forming and re-forming
over Copernicus's Tower.

I looked from the roof
till it was dark and starry, and I knew my travels
were just beginning: the Magellanic Clouds
wait for those who have climbed Magellan's shrouds.

Juggernaut
(1600 AD)

I had had enough of stars and silence.
It was midsummer, and I made for India.
Where would I get some life but India?
I joined a boat, and was soon blistering
across the Bay of Bengal to a seaside town
of some fame, what was it called, Puri,
yes, Puri of the festivals. A test case
I was told. Test of what? Oh you'll find out.

If I wanted people, there were plenty of them,
tens, hundreds of thousands, filling the streets
with chatter and movement and colour and slowly
making a magnet of the courtyard of a temple
where they clustered jostling in ancient expectation.
With a rumble, with shouts, with drums, with blowing of shells
an enormous cart rolled out, what, sixteen wheels,
a car for a god, a car for the people to draw,
and draw it they did, with their god on board,
that giant tottering legless fearsome one
they dragged as if drugged, they were high on devotion,
milling, chanting, pushing, stumbling, trundling –
trundling what, on those great spokes, to the sea?
I can hear the roar even yet, mounting up
through waves of heat and dust, it could curdle blood
or it could twine your roots with the roots of the world.
'Who is Lord of the Universe? Jagannath!
Who is Jagannath? Lord of the Universe!'

The juggernaut rolled on, and made its path
over so many bodies no one could say
who had been shouldered to the ground
or who had shouldered themselves to the ground,
embracing the relentless axle of the divine.
I could not say. I did not want to say.
Shining eyes, shouts of ecstasy,
stench, stampede, shattered shinbones,
sun–splashed awnings, sweat-soaked idols
swam before me like sharks, like shrieks
from an old incomprehensible abyss.

The axle squeals without redress of grease.

Easter Island
(1722 AD)

I write it, I read it, I revere that sea
which blues the heaving earthly hemisphere.
I was swooping low over those waves one day
when my eye caught a tiny triangle of island
some instinct told me to investigate:
volcanic, a mere scrub of greenery,
but interesting in its defiant aloneness
thousands of miles from the nearest land.
I spoke to the inhabitants. They were curious.
They were mighty voyagers, or their ancestors were,
not now though; there was some great past,
fragments only, drifting through memory.
I found them quite a merry people.
They preferred tattoos to clothes.
They shot their legs out in shameless dances.
What use is shame in mid-Pacific?

Whoever they were, they were not the ones
whose gaunt and awesome faces stared at – not me
but space and clouds and things unknown
unless to those who carved them.
Hundreds of statues, six-men-high and more,
standing, leaning, lying, trying
to break from the earth like Polynesian Adams –
but not Polynesian, they forbade identity:
pointed nose, thin lip, jutting chin
said nothing but Power! Mystery! Vision!
What force moved them from their quarries,
those many tons, across the rough of the island?
They were not moved, they moved, I was told.
Step by step, rocking from side to side,
they reached their appointed places.
Everyone knows that, I was told.

It was evening now, evening of what some would call
Easter Sunday. I climbed a hill near the coast,
gazing across those vast waters not vaster
than tracts of mind new-visited and glittering.
On the horizon, the first ship from Europe:
trinkets, missionaries, trousers, smallpox, guns.

The Lisbon Earthquake
(1755 AD)

A continent's western edge, high ships in harbour,
huge harbour it was too, a haven for all,
a hallowed circle for that All Saints' Day
of a still, half-gold, half-sombre November:
the bells clashed and clamoured, the churches were packed,
the candles were packed thick as forests, the voices
packed themselves into trembling glades of praise.
I watched it all, watched the end of it all.
The earth dreams like a dog in a basket,
twitching; it likes to show it is alive.
At the first tremor, people look at each other,
they are not fools, they know what is happening,
but with no more warning than a crash
the sculptured roofs fell on the worshippers,
leaving a squirm of screams, blood, blazing wax.
Those who could run, ran, ran to the sea
to save them, but save them it could not:
it rose in a wall of water, a wave of waves
that roiled and howled and brought a great drowning,
mantillas, black suits, copes of purple, swaddling-clothes.

That was a *fado*
singing, fading.
I heard it in the wailing of the wounded.
It rose like smoke from fires that would rage for days.
It tore the Enlightenment to tatters.
It made philosophers of men on stumps.
I saw a small crowd and spoke to them.
Throw away your candles, I said. It's a new age.
Study the earth. Listen to its plates grinding.
Power is yours, not up there – I pointed –
you have a long trek, and tears, but
it is your own trek, your own tears,
you must never freeze-frame your fears.
Clear the rubble. Mourn the missing.
Keep one ruin for remembrance sake.
Tell old Tagus a new Troy is at stake!

A woman nodded, took flowers, strode ahead.
It was November First, the Day of the Dead.

Darwin in the Galapagos
(1835 AD)

It was a cool day for the equator
as I clambered whistling over the clinker.
Clouds had brought a shower across the shore.
Grey black scoured and pitted rocks
glistened, and so did an iguana
eyeing me lazily with its wet crest bristling.
I saw the drag-marks of a giant tortoise –
what a dogged message thrusting into the thicket!
And the air was bright with birds, well, bright and dark –
green, brown, yellow – little birds, finches
flirting their few inches, drenching the freshness
with a spray of chatter and chirm, with a charm
peculiar to these islands, these Incantadas

I met a young man in a floppy hat
who stopped and smiled; he too had charm.
'My finches,' he said, 'you are watching my finches.'
We sat on an old stump, I cherish the moment.
A man both ingenuous and ingenious,
a genius indeed, enthusiastic, shy,
well no, not really shy, but modest,
that was a type I could talk to for ever.
'These finches – all different,' he said.
'They have become separate species, and why is that?
They had some ancestor in Ecuador
but here their beaks have changed to match their food –
small seeds, big seeds, nectar, and do you know
there is one that makes a tool of cactus spines
to ferret grubs from tree-cracks? Oh
I can hardly sleep for excitement!
Nothing is immutable, life changes, we evolve.
Process is gorgeous, is it not!
Process is progress, don't you see!'

He taps my arm, his eyes shine. I agree.
Time breaks in great waves as we speak.
And look, a finch on the back of a tortoise
as if it had been listening
lifts its beak and begins a singing
so piercing it gives no end to that beginning.

Rimbaud
(1891 AD)

A wheezing fan hardly disturbed the flies.
A crutch stood in the corner. Hoots from the harbour
brought Marseilles into a stifling hospital
where the gaunt drugged gun-runner lay
sweating and groaning with his bandaged stump
staining the sheets as he muttered and turned.
I listened. I knew who he was.
This dying trader had once been a poet.
Can you once be a poet, and live? Well, can you?
I wanted to swim in his delirium.
I did, I did swim in his delirium.

' – ten thousand rifles, they were all stacked
but I was swindled, Abyssinia swindled me,
is it slaves next, or stick to tusks and spices,
I can still ride the sands, trafficking trafficking,
get to the gulf, the sea, the green, oh my thirst,
I cannot drink, Venus with her green eyes
is rising from a green copper bath,
she is bald, larded, ulcered, she is dripping
with verdigris and I am thirsty I want I want
absinth, *absomphe*, my green, my demon, my dear,
and I am hungry but all I scrunch is coal and iron,
I even scrunch walls I am such a monster,
Djami, Djami, what sort of boy are you,
bring me my pipe, where is my white shirt,
you must not laugh at my grey hairs,
Paul, come back, I shall be good,
do you really believe you can ever
find anyone better to live with,
I shall jump on you, we shall roll together,
Paul, I need you, I love you,
the pain, this pain, someone is crunching my leg
in an iron boot, I expect it is God,
what are we born for, write poetry, nah – '

A wave of traffic broke loudly outside.
I wanted a wave of the sea, real air, gulls.
I left the sick smell and the old young man.
Poetry burned in him like radium.

The Siege of Leningrad
(1941–1944 AD)

Enormous icy Ladoga, lake for giants,
cracked quietly in the fog and under the cracks
artillery threw across a whistling darkness.
I hunched into my furs, made for the city.
On the outskirts, black figures crouched
to scoop up water from broken pipes
below the snow. Over the snow
sledges loaded with the dead
were dragged by the half-dead.
A gaunt dog slunk near. Bury them quick!
Hunger is in his ribs and he cannot howl
but he can eat! The millions besieged
can eat, five ounces of bread a day,
two glasses of hot water, a rat if caught,
then gnaw some leather, wrap in rugs,
wait for the droning overhead.

Music: what was that! I passed a hall,
peered in: huddled crowd, breath, baton,
dim flash of brass. Crashes of Shostakovich
crushed the frost and raced through the blood.
How could those hearts ever surrender?
Pinched noses and grey flesh, all right; they starved;
starved, thousands; but kept schools open,
hospitals, factories, pipeline under Ladoga,
Peter the Great's children, yes, Lenin's children,
say what you will, they held the line. They live
in the memory of poets and of those far ones
like myself who visit everything
but do not always stand in awe like this
as shells shriek through the innocent flakes
and print the north in blood.

                    I watched
wave after wave of bombers darken the sky.
That night the great observatory was hit.
The eye of Pulkovo searching for Barnard's Star
went blind as the lake its frozen companion
that guarded it and was guarded by it –
until the pain should be melted and the people
sing in the harmless moon of their white nights.

39

The Sputnik's Tale
(1957 AD)

One day, as I was idling above the earth,
an unexpected glint caught my eye,
whizzing silver, a perky sphere with prongs.
I knew it was time for such things to appear
but this was the first: man-made, well-made,
artificial but a satellite for all that:
a who-goes-there for the universe!
I came closer: the gleaming aluminium
sparkled, hummed, vibrated, its four
spidery antennas had the spring of the newly created.
It seemed a merry creature, even cocky.
It had a voice. I said hello to it.

'Can't stop,' it cried. 'I am in orbit.
Join me if you want to talk. *Beep.*
Travel with me, be the sputnik's sputnik.'
I flew alongside. 'What have you seen?' I asked.
'Wall of China, useless object that.
Continents. Tankers. Deltas like pony-tails.
Collective *beep* farms everywhere. Oh and
the earth like a ball, mustn't forget that,
proof positive. And a blue glow
all round it if you like such *beep* things.'

'You haven't always been bound in a bit of metal?'
I asked. 'Damn sure I *beep* haven't,' he replied,
colour chasing colour across his surface.
'I was a bard in the barbarous times,
Widsith the far-traveller. The world was my mead-hall.
Goths gave me gold. I blossomed in Burgundy.
I watched Picts prick *beep* patterns on themselves.
I sang to Saracens for a sweet supper.
I shared the floor with a shaman in Finland.
Good is the giver who helps the harper!'

'I have nothing to give you,' I said,
'but truth. You have three months to live
in this orbit, and then you are a cinder.'
He darkened. 'You may well be right.'
But remembering Widsith he flushed into tremulous light.
'We'll see. *Beep.* We'll see. *Beep.* We'll see.'

Woodstock
(1969 AD)

How many people can be happy?
How many people can be peaceful?
Half a million in that field full of folk
I counted as I wandered through the morning.
This was the Catskills, not the Malvern hills,
but something good was breathing there.
Was music the magic? A million eyes
lifted young faces to gantries and amplifiers
banked like some gigantic stage-set –
well, a stage-set it was, a self-written play
rocked in waves of rhythmic clapping,
whistles, announcements, cheers, planes passing.

Smokes were smoked and backs were stroked.
A man died and a child was born.
Adam and Eve stood naked in a brook.
I should put this in a book.

Rain game, oh did it, thunder and mud.
Put on ponchos, caps, capes!
Bless and exorcise the flood!
Navajo rain-chant sweeps the crowd.

Weather was not the climax though.
What were we all waiting for?
When the clouds had passed and the bands
and songs were ready to be packed away,
in the unspoken expectation, electric,
an instrument rose like a dragon,
a guitar spoke like a dragon.
Starry and scary was the jangled spangle,
not blazing with blandishments that banjaxed banner,
a banshee brandished it in the vanguard.
When Hendrix plucked, it was the mane of a lion.
His fingers did the work of several hands.
But through the growling and through the whining,
through the slurring and through the piping,
through the grovelling and through the soaring,
the tune kept surfacing
almost heartbreaking,
bright and fighting.

The Twin Towers
(2001 AD)

For the Mercantile Exchange and the Commodity Exchange,
for the Cotton Exchange and the Coffee Exchange,
for the Market Bar and the Sky Dive,
for the Windows on the World at the 107th floor,
for the Miró three-ton tapestry and the Calder stable mobile,
there was suddenly no more time, my friends,
there was suddenly no more space.

For those therein, my dears, for those therein
it was twisted metal, scalding jet fuel,
smoke, fire, fear, baffled frenzy.
I saw it, but you must imagine it.
Think of those who escaped stumbling down stairwells,
think of the ones who escaped only into the air,
leaping hand in hand from highest windows
to be broken rather than burned: the pity of that.
Can you think of the pilots too, in the last moments
of that accurate blaze of impact as the towers loomed –
were they praying, crying, shouting, silent, counting –
can you place that final union of flesh, steel, glass
in the scale of sublimity proper to terror –
high, is it not high? You must say so!

The shock-waves were a tocsin for the overweening imperium;
let them take note, let them think how others live.
But tall towers may be arrogant, or they may not.
I shall become very cross – oh yes, I can be –
if I hear the word Babel. Advocates of lowliness,
keep off, creep off! There is a soaring thing
you will never stunt or stamp into the earth.

Like the broken comb of a geisha girl
which she has angrily thrown onto the road,
the ruined shell of half a tower
stood rakish against the sky
as if it was the monument it should become,
to let cascades of fine black hair unbound,
cascades of unbound weeping, fall
onto that deadly desolate ground
for two thousand heads and more
that never will be found.

On the Way to Barnard's Star
(2300 AD)

I heard of a stramash in Ophiuchus.
The constellation, the spreadeagled hero
clutching his serpent, was pulsing and blushing
like a giant squid. What was going on?
I will tell you what was going on.
Worlds were being lost, were being born.
I tingled at news of an expedition.

We were a band bound for Barnard's Star,
the smouldering ruby, second nearest to earth,
cool, slow-burning, oh it will be around
long after this sun has run out of helium.
It had, or was about to have, a planet.
(Who can say what time is at such distances?)
We travelled not far off the speed of light –
six years in our lusty photon-rider
would take us to the coasts of the red one.
What did we talk of? What did we not?
Destiny and will, great darkness and great light,
the fiery train of knowledge, the pearl of hope.
Meteors swept past us like battle-shot.
Clouds of gas were almost forms – almost –
but there were no gods, and we had good
blood in our veins, in our good brains,
and in black places too, in memory,
it stiffened there, where there was no grace,
blood, spilt, never to be effaced.
We drank to the dead. We blessed the unborn.
The computer blew its extraordinary horn
to tell us we were arriving, had arrived,
in bursts, were slowing, were slewing
past the dull red glow of Barnard's Star
down to its planet, slowly, in blurts,
landing at last on waves of grass.

Like glass
the green blades never waved, a river
in the distance shone but never ran,
laburnum – it was not laburnum –
dropped hard gold. The powerless stillness
was waiting. Help it. 'Open the hatch,' I said.

Valentine Weather

Kiss me with rain on your eyelashes,
come on, let us sway together,
under the trees, and to hell with thunder.

Three Songs

The Red Coat

Cross the river in the rain
Can things ever be the same
Get the heart to tell the brain

Take your red coat like a lantern
Fly in front to damn the phantom
White not black your only magic

Sing out when you reach the wood
Is this where the angel stood?
Is there a word, is there a mood?

It's wet but I can see you still
Drops like snails on the window-sill
Tracks of love nothing can kill.

Knock at the Door

Run – run – don't wait –
Who wants to be late
If love is at the gate –

An asteroid's might
Knocking on the door of night
Could be the end, yes it might –

But just be ready
Steady or unsteady
Step light or heavy

Bang back the shutters
Swish back the curtains
Welcoming – utterly –

The Good Years

Wherever you are
You shall be my star
Flashing near or smouldering far

I am happy when I bask
In your light, all I ask
Is that you may bask

In mine and hear the sound
Of every salty fount
Fresh as fresh is found

Singing without tears
Clinging without fears
These the good years

Old Gorbals

Old Gorbals in his long black coat
muttered and stalked from room to room.
He kicked up dust, dead flies, newspapers,
a crumpled envelope or two.
There was no news, there was no message
in the stillness, no cat, no dog,
no voice to his 'Anybody there?'
Of course not, they've all gone, gone where?
He'll never know, the thread is snapped
that he held fiercely all these years.
He shakes his head, crosses a window
like a shadow. There was so much life!
He can't believe it has disappeared:
he hears the children running, shrieking,
sees the TVs glowing blue,
marvels at the rows, the language,
crash of bottles, slam of doors,
car-doors too, oh yes, look down
at taxi after taxi, all piled full
with the raucous hopes of a Saturday.
The lamplight in the street looked up
at many windows bright at midnight,
and even when curtains were snatched tight
you felt hearts beating and lips meeting
as private twenty storeys up
as in any cottage by the sea.
Old Gorbals flicked dust from his sleeve,
sighed a bit and swore a bit,
made for the stairs, out, looked back
at the grand tower, gave a growl,
and in a spirit of something or other
sprayed a wall with DONT FORGET.

1955 – A Recollection

First there was one,
then there were two,
now there is one,
when will there be none?

Step down slowly,
down into the cold,
old cold, eternal cold,
refrigerated cold,
with grim stiff guards
every few feet
even in their greatcoats
cold, cold –
our shuffling queue
silent, shivering,
awed a little,
believers and unbelievers
circling a shrine,
curious, peering,
cameras forbidden,
eyes and brain
fixing images
that startle, frighten,
fascinate finally –
the two undead
laid side by side,
Lenin yellowing,
showing his years,
Stalin still rosy
as if lightly sleeping –
the strangest tableau
you are likely to see
this side of the grave.
I pour the amber
of a poem over it.

First there was one,
then there were two,
now there is one,
when will there be none?

My First Octopus

'What's good? What's special?' I asked the waiter
swaying expertly along the corridor
of the Istanbul-Ankara express.
His black moustache and merry black eyes
were voluble: 'Oc'pus today, you try.
Not Greek oc'pus like rubber,
real Turkish, you see our wrestlers,
they strong, they live on oc'pus.'
'OK I'll try it.' And I must say
the strips were soft and succulent,
soused in herbs and butter, yes sir.
A good tip, and back to my window-watching.
Two hours later, I felt the octopus
uncurling, sending me messages.
The toilet was a hole in the floor.
Squatting at sixty is not so easy
but I got down, Moses, I got down.
Would I ever get up again?
I could see the headlines: FOREIGN POET
FREED BY FIREMEN AFTER BEING STUCK
IN TOILET-HOLE. Hilarious.
But all was well. Will-power
pushed me to my feet, and soon
we were roaring down to Ankara,
leaving a little oc'pus deposit
for whatever birds and beasts come sniffing
along the tracks to see what's discarded
by the majestic hunkers of humanity.

Boethius

'Even the thrush, garrulous among the trees,
Caught and caged, and cosseted to please
A room of folk, regaled with frisky seeds,
Bells, mirrors, all the honey it needs,
Twinkling fingers, voices cooing it to sing,
If once through the windows the winds should bring
Shifting shadows of leaves, O how it rages,
It scatters the well-meant seeds, nothing assuages
Its longing for the wild woods and the sky,
Nothing can stop its cry,
And yet the kindly jailers wonder why.'

Silvas dulci voce susurrat. So wrote
Boethius, caged in Pavia,
how many years, in chains,
ex-senator, ex-orator, ex-everything,
dignities and dignity swiped off,
tears not wiped off,
groaning alone unheard
by Theodoric on his throne.
Grim in iron or gold or in iron and gold
Gothic kings will not be told
how to rule Rome. Romans
will not pack senates; Goths will.
Boethius, you stub your toe on iron.
You have stumbled into displeasure.
Fate must fulfil.
Take a cell, a shirt, a pen. Amen.

Not quite amen.
They gave him chains, they gave him pain.
But in candled darkness he wrote a book
to question fate, to challenge desolation.
Spiteless, Christless, working through
to a 'Yes' at last, in his late late Latin,
it gave a god a labyrinthine chance
to make a case for present suffering,
eternal sufferance. We look askance
at its title, *The Consolation of Philosophy*.

That was a bravado to pique Theodoric.
Theodoric the Great was out of patience.
Theodoric had not heard of judicial murder
but used it well, issued his order
for a little torture, then execution.
There is no such thing as philosophy.
There is no such thing as consolation.
Tyrants have lapis lazuli and porphyry.
Prisoners, the iron and gold of indignation.

Charles V

Your roughest robe, your roughest rope,
give me, invest me, gird me close.
Shave my head, and give me bread,
a little bread, a little water.
Show me my cell and damp may it be.
If there is sacking, I'll sleep on that.
If there is not, I'll sleep on stone.
Good monks, if I should sleep too long,
beat me awake. Let truth be known,
I am suppliant who had a throne,
a thousand suppliants of my own.
I blaze with emeralds in my belt,
I strutted in an ermine stole,
I flashed my crown in Bologna town.
The Holy Roman Empire was mine,
Loyola up and Luther down.
I had all Europe at my feet
a while, a while.

               All's gone, all's done.
Cold slabs are at my feet. Bolts clang.
Empire of universal dreams,
Austria to America,
you are no more than the mirage
I saw in Africa, when Tunis shimmered
into Rome, and both into the dark.

Oscar Wilde

Up with their skirts, pointing, hooting,
oh yes, and one or two were spitting,
triumphalism of the whores,
rival of the flesh seen safely off
into the blue arms of the law –
that was not my favourite pavement.
Some saw it only as fair payment,
settling of accounts with decency.
Decent, indecent, who knows what that is?
A tin slittering the floor of the cell
with a whole night's pish from five to five?
A cold plank bed, a bowl of skilly?
How about a day's treadmilling,
a decent six hours to crack the muscles?
Decently dressed in the broad arrows
of humiliation, you cannot go wrong,
can you? go far, go back, can you?
Insomnia? Think about your sins.
Diarrhoea? You are full of shit.
I am thin, I am melancholy.
What is that light? I am squirming
like a pinned butterfly, still alive.
A visitor from France? I'm here,
humilié et anéanti. I am here.

Hirohito

Face? Lost face? What face? What loss?
Divine wind cannot kamikaze
emperors. Our face is in the stars.
If I am not divine, I am nothing.
I acted rightly, lord of these islands,
chastened China, pounded Pearl Harbor,
took all prisoners to be cowards, treated them
accordingly. To fear me was correct,
oppose impossible. I see no honour
except in Japan. I and honour rule.
What honour's in a mushroom cloud?
Honourable atom men, no thank you.
They, not we, are the yellow ones.
Safe in their droning planes they go
to hell.
        What's in that document?
Surrender? Never. Barbarians
east and west, clumsy white ones,
lords of nothing. What is that voice?
Kowtow? Fools, I am not Chinese.
– Kowtow! – Never! – It is the end of the line.
It is the end of the divine. Hear this.
You have knees, use them. Go down.
Forget your honour, save your life.
Kowtow. Sign! – Give me the pen.

New Times

Wave back, but they miss the mark.
Bended knee and corgi's bark
Peering north through churning dark

Will never cut it, now or finally.
So give us leave to build our highway
Which you may think is but a byway

But it is not. The general will
Is patient but asks us to fulfil
A fate that like a rugged hill

Is there for all to see; is seen;
Is acted on; we're raw, we're green,
But what's to come, not what has been,

Drives us charged and tingling-new,
To score our story on the blue,
Or if it's dark – still speak true.

Gorgo and Beau

GORGO, *a cancer cell*
BEAU, *a normal cell*

GORGO My old friend Beau, we meet again. How goes it?
    Howzit gaun? Wie geht's? Ça va? Eh?

BEAU Same old Gorgo, flashing your credentials:
    Any time, any place, any tongue, any race, you are there.
    It is bad enough doing what you do,
    But to boast about it – why do I talk to you?

GORGO You talk to me because you find it interesting.
    I am different. I stimulate the brain matter,
    Your mates are virtual clones –

BEAU   – Oh rubbish –

GORGO You know what I mean. Your paths are laid down.
    Your functions are clear. Your moves are gentlemanly.
    You even know when to die gracefully.
    Nothing is more boring than a well-made body.
    Why should this be? That's what you don't know.
    And that is why you want to talk to me.

BEAU You will never get me to abhor
    A body billions of us have laboured to build up
    Into a fortress of interlocking harmonies.

GORGO Oh what a high horse! I never said
    'Abhorrent', I said 'boring', not the same.
    Take a dinosaur. Go on, take a dinosaur,
    Tons of muscle, rampant killing-machine,
    Lord of the savannahs, *roars*, roars
    To make all tremble, but no, not anger,
    Not hunger fuels the blast, but pain –
    Look closer, watch that hirpling hip
    That billions of my ancestors have made cancerous,
    Deliciously, maddeningly, eye-catchingly cancerous.
    Not the end of the dinosaurs, I don't claim that,
    But a tiny intimation of the end

Of power, function, movement, and the beauty
That you would say attends such things.
Dinosaurs on crutches, how about that?

BEAU You think you can overturn pain with a cartoon?

GORGO Pain, what is pain? I have never felt it,
   Though I have watched our human hosts give signs –
   A gasp, a groan, a scream – whatever it is,
   They do not like it, and it must be our mission
   To give them more, if we are to prevail.
   But in any case what is so special about pain?
   Your goody-goody human beings, your heroes
   Plunge lobsters into boiling water – whoosh –
   Skin living snakes in eastern restaurants –
   Make flailing blood-baths for whales in the Faroes –
   What nonsense to think it a human prerogative,
   That pain, whatever it is. Not that I myself
   Or my many minions would refuse
   To make a camel cancerous, or a crab
   For that matter! First things first.
   Our empire spreads, with or without pain.

BEAU Shall I tell you something about suffering?
   Imagine a male cancer ward; morning;
   Curtains are swished back, urine bottles emptied,
   Medications laid out. 'Another day, another dollar'
   A voice comes between farts. Then a dance:
   Chemo man gathers up his jingling stand
   Of tubes and chemicals, embraces it, jigs with it,
   'Do you come here often?', unplug, plug in,
   Unplug, plug in, bed to toilet and back,
   Hoping to be safe again with unblocked drip.
   Afternoon: chemo man hunched on bed
   Vomiting into his cardboard bowl, and I mean vomiting,
   Retching and retching until he feels in his exhaustion
   His very insides are coming out. Well,
   That's normal. Rest, get some sleep.
   It's midnight now: out of the silent darkness
   A woman's sobs and cries, so many sobs,
   Such terrible cries; for her dying husband
   She arrived too late, she held a cold hand.
   The nurses stroked her, whispered to her,

Hugged her tight, in their practised arms.
But they could not console her,
She was not to be consoled,
She was inconsolable.
The ward lay awake, listening, fearful, impotent,
Thinking of death, that death, their own death to come
The sobbing ended; time for sleep, and nightmares.

GORGO Well now that's very touching I'm sure,
But let me open up this discussion.
I was flying over Africa recently
To see how my cells were doing, and while you
Were mooning over the death of one sick man
Lying well cared for in a hospital bed,
I saw thousands, hundreds of thousands
Massacred or mutilated, hands cut off,
Noses, ears, and not a cancer cell in sight.
Oh you bleeding hearts are such hypocrites!

BEAU Gorgo, you cannot multiply suffering in that way.
Each one of us is a world, and when its light goes out
It is right to mourn. And if the cause is known,
That you and your claws were scuttling through the flesh,
I call you to account. What are you up to?
Don't tell me you care about Africa.
Don't you want more wards, more weeping widows?

GORGO I want to knock you out, you and your miserable cohorts.
I want power. I am power-mad. No I'm not.
That's a figure of speech. I am not repeat not
Mad, but calculating and manipulative.
I am not at the mercy of blind forces.
You may think I am, but it is not so.
Consider: a tidy clump of my cells,
A millimetre long, a stupid mini-tumour,
Is stuck because it cannot reach its food,
It's lazy, dormant, useless and I can't stand
Uselessness. I help it to take thought.
It must expand. It can't expand.
It suddenly – and I mean suddenly –
Finds itself synthesising proteins
That generate blood-vessels, capillaries,
Tiny but broad enough for a breakthrough

Into nutrients, into voyages,
Into invasion and all that that implies.
Our human hosts are baffled: a thinking tumour?
Well, would you prefer an effect without a cause?

BEAU You could say something about this, I'm sure.

GORGO Could, but won't. There's a war on, you know.

BEAU Justify your armies, justify your battles.

GORGO Did you not hear what I said about power?
    Are your ears clean, or you keep them half-closed
    Against infection from a satanic tempter?
    You may not even think I am a tempter,
    But I am the insidious one, hissing Listen listen.
    Every tumour begins with a single cell
    Which divides and divides and is its own boss.
    It laughs to feel its freedom, to hell with blueprints,
    It shoulders and jostles its way in the organ-jungle.
    Even on a glass in the lab it's huddling and layering
    Like caviar, and does caviar have to justify
    Its juicy rolling formless proliferations?
    The joy of kicking decent cells away,
    Sucking their precious nutrients, piercing
    Membranes that try to keep you from the waves
    Of lymph and blood you long to navigate –
    Through unimaginable dangers, be robust! –
    Until you reach those Islands of the Blest –
    I hear you snort, Beau, don't explode! –
    The distant organs where you plant your flag
    And start a colony. Those cells are heroes,
    Homer would hymn them, but I do my best!

BEAU Heroes! If anything so small can be a monster,
    That's what you and your mates are. You sound like –

GORGO Forgive the interruption. I have a few words
    On monsters to give you later. Carry on –

BEAU – sound like Jenghiz Khan at the sack of Baghdad –

GORGO – at least he got into the history books –

BEAU Will you let me *speak*?

GORGO   All right all right.
    But I know what you are going to say.

BEAU You do not, but even if you did
    It would be worth saying. Imagine the baby
    Still in the womb, the image screened by ultrasound
    Flickering and shifting, not sharp but unmistakably
    Alive, the soft hand at the mouth, the dome
    Above it, that forehead of a million secrets
    Waiting to be born, everything vulnerable
    To the last degree, but with the strength
    That attends vulnerability in its beginnings.
    It grows, it emerges, it grows, not a single
    Bad gene in its body (your turn to snort,
    All right Gorgo, but listen, listen now).

GORGO (*sings*) The oncogene, the oncogene, it squats in the DNA
                    As proud and mim as a puddock, and will not go away.
    – Sorry, Beau. Continue.

BEAU As I was saying, imagine his growth,
    He is strong, well formed, not brilliant but bright,
    Explores the sea-bed, writes a book, has children,
    Tells them stories sitting on the terrace.
    Vibrations of health and harmony
    Are like a talisman he gives back to nature.
    His cells are in order, dying when they should.
    He measures power by love, given and taken.
    Your power does not tempt him.

GORGO   So Pollyanna
    Put on her skis, and was never seen again.
    It is a nice picture, but you made it all up.
    If there are such people, I must see what I can do
    To infiltrate, subvert, and overthrow them.
    Health and harmony? What a yawn.
    I promised you a word on monsters.
    I was helping one day to tie a knot
    In a long tumour which had got itself twisted
    (Deliberately, I'm sure) like a Möbius strip
    In a body cavity of a pleasant young woman:

60

She was flapping and shrieking on the hospital bed
In what I imagine was very great pain.
Doctors brought students, teratologists were tingling.
There was a sharp ferocity in the air
That put all thoughts of the ordinary to flight.
– A microscope will show you a different monster:
A nucleus too gigantic for the cell,
Ragged, pulsing, encroaching, a bloodshot eye
Staring at a wreckage of filaments and blobs,
Bursting with DNA, breaking apart
In a maelstrom of wild distorted chromosomes –
That was a sight to make you think, friend Beau!

BEAU I am thinking, of how these observations
Have twisted your mind like the tumour you described.
It is death to want to make the abnormal normal.
Suppose you and your assiduous myrmidons
Had made a body into one whole tumour,
Pulsating on a slab like a Damien Hirst exhibit,
A gross post-human slug, a thing of wonder,
What then? It dies, it is not immortal.
Preserve it? Mummies tell the future
How terrible the past was. Your goal and god
Is death, and that is why I oppose you.

GORGO And how will you get rid of me,
If it is not too delicate a question?

BEAU There's always regular hormone injections –

GORGO – make you fat and sexless –

BEAU A pinpoint zap with radiotherapy –

GORGO – leaves you tired and listless –

BEAU The swirl and drip of chemotherapy –

GORGO – you're sick as a dog and your hair falls out –

BEAU How about nano-bullets of silica
Plated with gold and heated with infra-red light –

GORGO – oh please –

BEAU Plants offer extracts; they get cancer too,
    So they should know what they are talking about.
    (*sings*) Sow periwinkle and the mistletoe,
            For these are fields where cancer cannot grow.

GORGO – you've got a point there –

BEAU Of course we are living now in a New Age –

GORGO – this should be hilarious –

BEAU Since mind and body can scarcely be separated,
    We shall not cease from mental fight etcetera.
    I can see my cells as nimble stylish knights
    While yours are clumsy dragons on the prowl.
    I can see my tumour as an old bunch of grapes
    From which I pick one rotten fruit each day
    Until the bad cells have all got the message
    And shrivel into invisibility.
    Some take it further; if there are good vibrations
    There must also be bad. How come you got the cancer
    And not Mr Robinson down the road?
    You must have self-suppressions, inhibitions,
    Guilts black or bleak or blistering, promises unkept,
    Hatreds unspoken, festering coils
    With their fangs and toxins destabilising
    Cells that are as open to emotion as to disease.
    If you want to dip further into the cesspit of causes,
    Remember those who believe in reincarnation.
    You send a poison-pen letter in one life
    And in the next it's returned with a sarcoma –
    Consequences are not to be escaped!
    What think you of all this, friend Gorgo?

GORGO I think it is nonsense and I don't believe it.
    Mind you, if it was true, I've no complaint
    When disillusioned visualisers
    Still sick, or more sick, go suicidal.

BEAU I don't believe it either, but I'm loath
    To brush any possibility aside.

In Celtic tradition, poets had the power
(It is said) to rhyme an enemy to death.
He was attacked in ruthless public verse,
And through suggestion and fear did actually
Fall ill and die. Cases are recorded.

GORGO I must watch what I say.

BEAU You take it lightly, but there are mysteries –

GORGO Of course there are mysteries. I give you leave,
    Indeed I encourage it, to examine everything,
    Fact, rumour, faith, fantasy, cutting edges
    Of science (pretty blunt cut so far),
    Cutting edges of imagination (look: a tumour transplant!).
    I am so confident, *we* are so confident,
    We black sheep are so confident (and remember
    Black sheep are natural) that we challenge you
    To ever catch up as we race ahead.
    I said there was a war on, and so there is,
    But let me recommend William Blake to you:
    'Without contraries is no progression.'
    Where would medical science be without us?

BEAU So pain, suffering, fear, death, bereavement
    Are grist to the mill of the universe,
    And the devotees of progress cry with joy
    As Juggernaut crushes them in its murderous wheels
    Down to the sea?

GORGO   Is it monsters again?
    You are overheated. Think calmly. Thank me
    For opening many secrets of the body.
    Thank me for forcing your thought into channels
    Of what is at once minute and vast speculation,
    Our place, your place, in the scheme of things,
    Should there be a scheme of things, which I doubt!
    My hordes, my billions, my workers
    Have added imperfection to any design
    You might impute to some beneficence –
    Beneficence without maleficence, no go! –
    You'll find us in the elephant, the cricket,
    The flatworm, the pine-tree, not stones yet

But who knows? Medieval spheres
Gliding on crystal gimbals could not last.
The rough inimical perilous world is better.
We rule; you rule; back and forward it goes.
Your hosts, your victims, have their obituaries
Closed in the figure of a hard-fought fight.
I leave you with the thought that we too,
We wicked ones, we errant cells
Have held our battleground for millions of years,
Uncounted millions of years.

BEAU The past is not the future. We are ready
To give you the hardest of hard times.
My host is walking gently in the sun.
Will you grit your teeth, and think of her?
We shall surely speak again. Arrivederci.

If mony a pickle maks a puckle
Does mony a mickle mak a muckle?
If we are aw Jock Tamson's bairns
Whit's the pynt o biggin cairns?
If yir face is trippin you
Zat mean it's really cripplin you?
Let that flee stick tae the waw –
Wull it no come aff an aw?
Zeenty teenty tethery dumpty –
Kin ye no say wan two three, ya numpty?
If sumdy cries, Yir baw's on the slates,
Dae ye luk fur a ledder or pit oan yir skates?
If facts are chiels that winna ding
Dae dreams no go their dinger an sing?
They say a gaun fit is ay gettin:
D' ye think aik an yew stert sweatin?
Better a wee bush than nae bield:
Bare-scud Picts on the battlefield?
Speak o the Deil an he appears.
Speak o Gode – nae fears, nae fears!

Questions II

What is that gorgeous blue gold-bordered gown, if it is a gown, doing as it
    folds and unfolds itself above the rooftops?

It is waiting impatiently for a poet to draw the sunset down to earth and
    put it on and join the ball of all.

Is it a dance? Can you hear the music? Have you got the beat?

Of course we hear the music and the beat is loud and sweet and our feet
    are on the street.

Is it a dance of earth and sky, and why?

Yes it's a dance of earth and sky and I don't know why, but you must keep
    asking!

Why?

Because the universe goes from door to door begging for questions. It
    hates a sullen tongue. It has unimaginable riches – except that it wants
    you to imagine them,

Are you trying to tell me that an awesome muster of galaxies, throbbing
    and spinning its glamour of dust and hydrogen and fire, is nothing but
    a beggar on the doorstep?

Yes. Think about it. Your very question is a step forward. How can it be,
    etcetera. I like that. Strike the paradoxes together and wait for the
    flame.

Did things begin, and will they end?

Take it to yourself that the double answer is no, and start from there.

What is blue?

I think I can say that blue is very good.

And gold?

Low in the west, in the evening, it will not harm you.

Can children join the dance?

Of course. Children are very good.

But are there not some bad children?

No no no. There are burrs of badness that come flying through the air and
    attach themselves to children – you must pick them off!

Why should a dog, a horse, a rat have life, and thou no breath at all?

Ah, you have that great dark questioner, King Lear, with his dead
    daughter in his arms. Why indeed? Let no minister or priest or rabbi
    or imam palm you off with a tale of 'if we knew the whole story,
    everything would fall into place'. Perhaps it would, perhaps it
    wouldn't! But take nothing on trust. Keep pushing the questions, and
    it may be that someday some sharply piercing query will open the
    tiniest of chinks in the lattice and let a star of light shine through.

Will it?

I said maybe. But never ask, never find.

The Welcome

A fanfare for librarians, in verse –
With no bum notes, whether florid or terse –
That's what the poet engages to deliver,
The word-enroller and the rhythm-giver.
Books have come and gone and come again,
Though some are written by a virtual pen.
Guard your Elzevirs, but also log
Titles from Pantagruel's catalogue:
The Bagpipe of the Prelates, The Ape's Paternoster,
Or any other monster from the roster.
Borges thought the great starry array,
The universe, was but a library.
Muster and master its infinite folios
And you could think you knew what no one knows.
We want it all; the universe itself
Expands, shelf beyond Hubble-bubbling shelf!
Starbursts of outreach – access – information –
We're on the very edge of a space station
Where ignorance will not be bliss but drastic,
Where learning curves must learn to be elastic,
Where we must search, and find, and use the things
That our search engine – oh, be patient! – brings.
Digitise a gilded Book of Hours,
It's not the same, but there it is, it's ours,
And long-dead times revive and look at us
As we interrogate their calculus.
Page or tape or disk or means unknown
Lie in wait wherever light is thrown,
To spread that light for everyone to see
And step by step enter immensity.

Glasgow, London, Europe, everywhere –
The poet's words may vanish into air
But they are words of welcome. May your meetings
Flourish braced by good old Mungo's greetings.
Perhaps he hears you, snoring by the Clyde,
With tree and bird, fish and bell at his side.
Well, you may find his story in a book,
In a library, if you know where to look.
From Mungo's cell to cyberspace, reality

Is a tango of intertextuality.
Have a fine dance with it this week, unlock
Your word-hoards, take heart and take stock
Of everything a library can do
To let the future shimmer and show through.

Brothers and Keepers

It was heard all right; that was not the argument.
Day or night it echoed from wall to wall,
A voice, never incomprehensible,
But a question many found intolerable:
'Am I my brother's keeper?' Some with scorn,
Some with anger, some with quick dismissal
Some with the half-uneasy consciousness
Of being put on the spot, some blustering,
Some brazen, some bound to macho boasts,
Kicking the can of pity out of play,
'Each to his own, let them get on with it!'

Conflicting shouts and voices did not stop us.
Threats were grist to the mill. We wanted
The record of what was and is and may be
To be set down if not in letters of fire
At least in good black print and clicks of mouse
To open up what's wrong, what's right, texting,
Probing, shaming, dreaming, countering
The last indifference.
        Who could be indifferent
When we took psychotic Steve from his filthy bolthole
Into a modest hostel room and he murmured
In half-belief 'Is this all for me?'
The reward of gratitude is a star in dark skies.
You cannot always help but trying is the crux.
I well remember that old alky Bill
Who shared his hovel of a house with others;
They held him prisoner among the litter
Of needles and syringes and empty bottles
Waiting to be smashed on social workers.
Another place for Bill? – possible,
But he's a bloody mess from fights at the moment.
We don't give up, that nothing is easy
Makes it even better not to give up.
Everyone alive is subject to change.
Hope lies where you least expect it.
Take exclusion from school, or rather don't take it!
Sandra, a so-called impossible child,
Made sure each class was disrupted to breaking-point.

Yelling, hitting, throwing chairs about,
Was she getting what she wanted,
Did she know what she wanted,
Was it 'What is to be done with her?'
Or rather 'What has been done to her?'
She was a child abused, her mother on drugs,
She had become a 'case', found caring arms
In social services alone, and there
Not only care but cure: a worker assigned
To be with her throughout school, helping, calming,
A bridge of sympathy between teacher and pupil,
A dedication not all that far from love.
Homelessness is terrible, but a home
Without love is almost equally so.
We watch, we measure, we praise whatever
Society can do, given the means and the people
To unknot fearful twists of fate, each day
Brings more, and if we are powerless
We cry out in our powerlessness.
If we are to blame, then we are to blame;
Fair treatment is what we ask.
                            My friends,
There is always without doubt a worst case,
And it is so bad because it is so rare,
Call it the dark night of the carer's soul.
Here you have Carl, supreme in cunning,
Known to have a personality disorder,
But showing the social team 'continued improvement':
Ah what a quiet mockery he made
Of schizophrenia! This man, however,
Took a claw hammer to his next victim's head,
Fried his brain with butter and ate it –
'Very nice,' he said. And unpredictable
One might add, although social workers
Would still have nightmares, thinking, shivering –
What was needed other than what they had,
Vigilance to the last degree, happy recall
Of those so many they had helped, brought back
To life with faith and hope blessedly renewed.

Oh if you ever thought we were not required,
Workers on the very edge of despair,
Consider Joe, kicked out by foster-carers

At twelve, having stolen from the little they had:
'Ah don't know why Ah done it, but it's okay
If they didny wahnt me back, it's okay –
My ma didny wahnt me either.' To live
In such unquestioned acceptance of defeat
Is dreadful, yet we know Joe can be helped.
The value of a soul can be drawn out
By those who are trained to do so, those
Who can blow the tiniest downtrodden spark
Of self-esteem into flame. You drop a tear
In instant sympathy or you are filled
With anger against systems and perpetrators,
And this is good and fine and natural.
But change is all the practicalities
Of learning, funding, understanding, change
Is everything we believe to be possible,
Whatever the squalor and sickness and stink.

There will never be a paradise with people like angels
Walking and singing through forests of music,
But let us have the decency of a society
That helps those who cannot help themselves.
It can be done; it must be done; so do it.

The Old Man and E.A.P.

He is not sleeping, though you might think so.
His eyes are half shut against the light.
'An old man's nap.' They smile, walk softly on.
He is smiling too, but mentally.
Without a twitch, he is on dragonback
above Edgarallanwood – what's in a name –
getting ready to rein in on the low moon.
It was a certain very dark exhilaration
played invisibly along his lips,
or a dark pride in riding such a beast
perched among its spikes and rolling folds
as it swished through cypresses, topped them,
kicked them, flicked them with a thundery tail
out below back down into men and
all that, last dog-walk of the day, hurrying,
whistle and whoop through Edgarallanwood.

He is full of questions, this man who is not sleeping.
Ever since the Fall of the House of Answer –
what's in a name – he has kept a brace
of dragons, dangling like markers in a diary,
whiffling at him as if they had the speech
of old times; he listens, hard, hard,
asks them in all the languages he knows
if there was a day, if there could have been a day,
if there was ever a night or a day
when they conversed with human kind, guarded
on terms of equality with ungreedy heroes
the well-locked unimaginable treasuries
laid up from times still older, and what
oh what would those times have been like, he asks.
The dragon's ear is dumb; it blinks; it hits
the moon, its wings are white with dust, the ages
dissolve in airless silence. Go on, bark,
last dog of evening, open the man's eyes.
'Had a good nap?' He smiles. 'Better than that:
I sprang a tale of mystery and imagination.'

An Old Woman's Birthday

That's me ninety-four. If we are celebrating
I'll take a large Drambuie, many thanks,
and then I'll have a small one every evening
for the next six years. After that – something quick
and I'll be off. A second century doesn't entice.
When I was a girl, you thought you would live for ever.
Those endless summer twilights under the trees,
sauntering, talking, clutching a modest glass
of grampa's punch diluted to suit young ladies –
diluted? It didn't seem so! The crafty old man
loved to see us glowing, certainly not swaying
but just ever so slightly, what do you say, high.

Life put all that away. I drove an ambulance
through shells, ruins, mines, cries, blood,
frightful, days of frightfulness who could forget?
It is not to be dwelt on; we do what we can.
If this is hell, and there is no other,
we are tempered, I was tempered – fires, fires –
I was a woman then, I was not broken.
No angel either; the man I married knew that!
Well, we had our times. What are quarrels for
but to make amends, get stronger. We did, we were.
He is gone now. I don't have a budgie in a cage
but I am one, and if you want me to sing
it will take more than cuttlebone and mirror:
more than Drambuie: more than if there was ever
good news out of Iraq where my ambulance
would keep me day and night without sleep:
more than what I say here, sitting
waiting for my son to come and see me
perhaps with flowers, chocolate, a card,
oh I don't know, he is late, he is ill,
he is old, I forget his heart is worse
than mine, but still, I know he'll do his best.

You really want me to sing? Come on then,
you sing first, then a duet, I love a duet.

For David Daiches, on his Ninetieth Birthday

'He must be ninety if he's a day' –
That's what I heard Methuselah say
As he scoured the Internet with a glint
(Not nine hundred yet though, eh?).
'The boy is coming on. Let's print
Congratulations in hard copy,
Nothing stinted, nothing sloppy!'

David in his youth combined
Dreams of an undivided mind,
Sprezzatura of the chanter
Solemn sadness of the cantor.
Travelling salesmen spliced his ears
Like weird Scots-Yiddish balladeers:
'Aye man, ich hob' getrebbelt mit
De midday train.' A fuse was lit
To language, culture, history, nation,
Whatever needed validation
Circled by imagination.
He swept up Burns, Fergusson, Scott,
And Andrew Fletcher who cursed the knot
Of Union, cursed his land and told it
'Was only fit for the slaves who sold it'.

The spirit of that land survived
In senses you may think contrived,
But David takes this in his stride
And casts his net both deep and wide.
A spirit well distilled, unique,
Fragrant as mist, treasure to seek –
David has pressed this in his book.
Beside the Taj Mahal he shook
The moonlight with a classic swig:
Glenlivet, rosier than the Rig-
Veda to a wanderer's soul!
Keep our tempers hale and whole!

David, but not our David, danced,
We are told, before the Lord
With all his might, like one entranced,

In a white smock without a cord,
While shouts and trumpets brought the ark
To blare and brilliance from the dark.

Our David wanted to throw light
On many: got them in his sight
As critic, not to shoot them down
Or crack their brows into a frown
Of Derridean doubts – or douts.
He set small store by sparring-bouts
But targeted coherences.
He gave MacDiarmid, Milton, Moses
More than flash appearances;
There was a web, a net, a gnosis
That could not be described, but felt,
Whatever Queens of Spades were dealt.

David, your friends are gathered here
To celebrate your latest year
Within a life led well and long.
This is a poem, not a song,
But you may hear it like the dear
Strains King David danced among.

A Birthday: for I.H.F.

It is no use offering the gatekeeper a garland of seventy-nine
          rhododendron petals. He can count.
Do not waste your time showing the guardian of the grove a
          pretty pretty book of eighty-one amorous pictures.
And as for that album of seventy-eight famous executions,
          keep it for the next bonfire.
If you are ever tempted to photograph a convocation of eighty-two
          midges thin with hunger and thirst, forget it.
Or if the cosmetic surgeon from Giacometti & Co. promises
          to make you a new man on payment of only
          seventy-seven pounds sterling, turn your pockets out
          with a shrug.
But when at last you come across the ship with eighty
          sails, oh what a sight that is to take to heart, with
          the white canvas flapping and the rigging snapping as
          she churns the ocean through a stiff breeze, and the
          sailors sing out their seemingly inexhaustible store
          of shanties, and the dolphins slice and gleam
          and are ahead of the prow like protective things
          from a world that is not quite ours, and the
          playful captain out of sheer joy blasts his
          horn eighty times into the misty morning, and
          then with his blue eyes glittering he bangs the
          rail – 'Steady as she goes!'

Wild Cuts

by Edwin Morgan and Hamish Whyte

Natural Philosophy

The dim shadow
  of the thing
was but a blur
against the dim shadows
  of the woods behind it.

A Bird Too Many

Notwithstanding
his suffering
he found himself smiling
as he contemplated the remnant
of his long-suffering
ducks.

Sure of a Big Surprise

She dared not again
tempt fate
in the gloomy wood
by night.

A Drip Too Many

About it the liquids of
decomposition had killed
vegetation, leaving the thing
alone in all its grisly
repulsiveness as though shocked
nature had withdrawn in terror.

Soothe and Improve

He knew little more of savage dances
than his tribesmen did
of the two-step and the waltz;
but he knew that dancing
and song and play
marked in themselves
a great step upward.

A Whizz Too Many

A haze obscured his vision –
everything became black – his brain
was whizzing about at frightful velocity
within the awful darkness of his skull.

Last Days

  man moved less rapidly
and as he went
he looked now for a burrow
into which he might crawl

A Movement Too Many

Presently the smoke came out,
as I have told you,
and the cliff went away
toward the edge of the world.
But they are all dead now.

(Found poems from Edgar Rice Burroughs, *The Cave Girl*, 1913)

Five Paintings

Salvador Dali: Christ of St John of the Cross

It is not of this world, and yet it is,
And that is how it should be.
Strong light hits back and the arms
Coming from where we cannot see,
Ought not to see, another dimension
For another time. At this time, we
Share the life of bay and boat
With simply painted fishermen
Who would give no Amen
Even if clouds both apocalyptic and real
Made them look up and feel
What they had to feel
Of shattering amazement, fear,
Protection, and a wash of glory.
Was it an end coming near?
Was it a beginning coming near?
What happened to the thorns and blood and sweat?
What happened to the hands like claws the whipcord muscles?
Has the artist never seen Grünewald?
'I have to tell you John of the Cross called,
Said to remind you light and death once met.'

Sir Henry Raeburn: Portrait of Rev. Robert Walker Skating
on Duddingston Loch

The skating minister is well balanced
And knows it. Something distinctly smug
Keeps those arms in place. Wouldn't it be good
If the god of thaws pulled that icy rug
From under him, to remind his next sermon
What it is that goeth before a fall.
He shivers before the fire
Hunched in his wife's mocking shawl –
Not the thing at all!

Rembrandt: Man in Armour

No warrior here.
This is a man who has put on some armour
In the cause of art. No enemy is near,
The helmet is well burnished and no doubt,
If tapped, gives off a musical note.
It would certainly not
Smudge hand or glove with caked or dusty blood.
If the man is faintly smiling, that would fit.
Rembrandt, man, everyone will love it.

Bring back your son, yourself, the woman at her bath,
And we'll use words like masterpiece again,
A cupboard is the best place for jingle-jangle.
Oh it's well done: the head looms out of darkness
With all the accoutrements bar pain.
You are great; even a loss from you's a gain.
But do not trivialise the death of men.

Joan Eardley: Flood-Tide

Lonely people are drawn to the sea.
Not for this artist the surge and glitter of salons,
Clutch of a sherry or making polite conversation
See her when she is free:
Standing into the salty bluster of a cliff-top
In her paint-splashed corduroys,
Humming as she recalls the wild shy boys
She sketched in the city, allowing nature's nations
Of grasses and wild shy flowers to stick
To the canvas they were blown against
By the mighty Catterline wind –
All becomes art, and as if it was incensed
By the painter's brush the sea growls up
In a white flood.
The artist's cup
Is overflowing with what she dares
To think is joy, caught unawares
As if on the wing. A solitary clover,
Unable to read WET PAINT, rolls over
Once, twice, and then it's fixed,

Part of a field more human than the one
That took the gale and is now
As she is, beyond the sun.

Avril Paton: Windows on the West

Turn the kaleidoscope and the seventy-eyed creature
Stretches, yawns, shakes the roof snow
Off its back in clumsy dollops, gets a glow
Going, cries of 'It's freezing!' (not really, just a feature
Of tenement winter), puts some coffee on, come on –
How can a single one be a multiple seventy –
I don't know, but I know I like the mystery –
Breathe out, breathe in, never in unison –
'When did you get in last night?' – 'Where the hell
Did you put my razor?' – 'Dog has started
To chew things up again' – 'Well well,
You were going to give it a bone, that's your department' –
'That was never what art meant,
Pictures falling off the wall, everyone has a –'
'Don't throw it away. I might need it' –
'You'll never write a line if you don't heed it
When I tell you there's enough life,
Enough strife
In this old sandstone block
To turn *Anna Karenina* and *The Great Gatsby*
Into one noble undefeated cry
Which is the single tenement sigh
Any time, anywhere.
Turn up the heat,
A new day's always sweet.'
'Coffee up.'
'My god another cracked cup.'

Love and a Life

Those and These

Frank, Jean, Cosgrove, John, Malcolm, Mark – loves of sixty years
Were a life that disported itself in many wonders not dispirited, though
     fears
Visited often, and were there not (said Mark) other dears
Like Leila who clutched your crotch in Cairo in '41, she just disappears
Is that it? And the night you broke the bed out there (said Malcolm), too
     many beers –
       Are you airbrushing a face,
       A grace, a disgrace –
No no I'm not, they are all there, crowding round me, others, milling,
     mingling, tingling, tangling, pinning me, pulling my ears.

Freeze-Frame

None of those once known is disknown, hidden, lost, I see them in clouds
     in streets in trees
Often and often, or in dreams, or if I feel I ought to be at my ease
They prod and probe: 'When my head was on your knees
And your hand was on my head, did you think time would seize
Head, hand, all, lock all away where there is no ring of keys –?'
       I did not, oh I did not,
       But look what I have got,
Frame of a moment made for friendless friendly time to freeze.

The Top

What use is a picture when the universe is up and drumming
With its passions motions missions misprisions relentlessly going and
    coming
Ghostly file of memories mopping and mowing and mumming –
In their hands a brilliant top that they lash and lash to release its
    humming –
It spins whistling softly until it wobbles, and you speed it with one last
    angry thumbing
        But soon it must fall back
        Into silence, attack
As you will, take the lash as you will, to stave off the mundane numbing
    and dumbing.

Tracks and Crops

Memory is not a top that never stops, but there is such a top, top of the tops,
Call it a world, it's drenched with what you did, it grins and groans with
    the drips and drops
Of your life, the sweat the blood the wine the weeping the honey and the
    hops,
Whatever you squeezed or poured or distilled or scrambled from pores or
    veins, elixirs, poisons, potions not filched from shops –
A bloom or glow like the first faint stirring of earthly unearthly crops –
        The cosmic harvesters
        Are scouring the universe
For sheafs and tracks of love left well by all from lucky you to luckless but
    once-loved horny veggie triceratops.

Jurassic

I have a dinosaur egg in my cupboard, hard, heavy, fused to the rock it
     haunts.
Someday Mark will have it and tempt its Jurassic chirp with his shazams
     and taunts.
Love laid the egg even in those armoured times when the bellows and vaunts
Of the laithly saurians belted out their ancient unlaithly wants –
(And tenderly our own dear crocodile conveys her squeaking brood in jaws
     no buffalo daunts) –
        Some malice surely must
        Have sent the deadly dust
That smothers what the pregnant earth gigantically flags up and flaunts.

Crocodiles

Patient patient men who can make pets of crocodiles
Disclaim they have degrees in sedation or access to preternatural wiles.
'It's touch,' they say. 'If you know where to press, that's good; if not, not!
     There are no smiles
(Don't be misled!), no purrs, no contented sighs to help you. Forget the
     styles
Of furry bundles. Communicate far back and down, then further back and
     further down, eras, miles.
        Expressionlessness
        Has ports of ingress –
Enter, clasp, hug, and then how quickly the esteemed veneer resiles!'

Touch

Touch is everything or nearly everything or it is nothing. Crocodiles mate,
    after all.
The Devil's swedger at minus a hundred is as cold and as ruthless as the Pole
And only the most despairing and abandoned, female or male, could take it
    in their hole
Or so we were told, or so they were told, when wretched creatures were
    taught of the Fall
Of Man instead of the Rise of Man and hair-shirts and chastity-belts were
    thought to assist our feeble but our dearest soul
        Which struggled, crying, to be free
        And use its body to be
The means of greatest grace, frolicking and fucking in the tropical
    throbbing unstoppable waterfall.

Night Hunt

The waters fall, and under the steelbright moon the hunters and the
    hunted shake the shadows in their trackless well-tracked wood.
The barred and silvered dark is like a gateless cage crammed full of living
    food.
Food for living! It cowers but you have to snatch it, crunch it, get it down
    your throat for good.
Who can say blameworthy bloodweltering nature is anxious to be
    understood?
Well, nothing is worthy of blame that feeds the root of bud baby and brood.
        It's a darkness all the same,
        Coming to light in the shame
Of knowing we would probably not banish our misgivings, even if we could.

Under the Falls

Break through and down with you, lovers all, down but not dry behind the
      falls.
You're staring into a rainbow spray, an unstrung bead-curtain as ready to
      brush breasts as any in cool levantine halls.
The loud fresh swish and rush, the flash, the drizzle disorientates as well
      as enthrals.
You sit back in a limbo cave of wonder, imagining the bird-calls
Whistling through a paradise garden where all that falls
           Is a loved footfall
           Hardly disturbing at all
The green and drowsy floor, and a world stretches somewhere, unseen,
      without woes or walls.

An Early Garden

My grandmother had a garden where I played as if arrayed in the heady
      scents of other days –
Sweet pea mignonette wallflower phlox – recollection sees them shining in
      rainless summer rays
Blooming and wafting for ever, and in the absence of roses demanding
      special praise.
I remember roses much later, but in that early garden their erotic blaze
Would have broken the innocence of such a mixed sweet haze
           When I dreamed of lands
           Untouched by hands
And drifted along even greater multi-scented ways where nothing, except
      a lucky memory, stays.

A Garden Lost

Maud never came into the garden: the fool was ower blate!
She thought the poet's deep voice and floppy hat were great
But oh, the garden was squishy with worms and slugs and pigeons would
    mate
Before her eyes and a cobwebby shed would relate
Either silence or old horrors. Well, one day they padlocked the gate
        And she looked in and cried
        'Oh I could have tried!'
But love is not invited twice and longing comes too late.

Beyond the Garden

When they lock the garden you go out into tumbleweed and sidewinder
    land.
You stumble a bit, curse a bit, thirst a bit until you see you have to settle
    into the ways of sand.
Date palms and desert springs, find them; eat lizards; understand
Every dust-devil may disgorge an afreet, no demon is banned
In the wilderness; keep watch; keep sane. Dunes, yes, on this strand
        But they don't show you a sea
        And you must learn to be
As dry as a scorpion, or a burr in the sand-golden tresses of Fand.

Cape Found

After how many days, how many months, we heard the waves, and sand
    became rock, and rock fell into the sound
So far below we hesitated but did call it Cape Found.
It was a great bay full of whales blowing. From our cliff the whole earth
    seemed round.
We clambered down to the machair and jumped on the springy half-
    soaked blessed ground.
'Do you remember the *Heiliger Dankgesang*?' 'Bits.' 'Sing some.' The frail
    notes rose and crowned
        Our passage back to men,
        To women, to children,
To ships and sails of health, to the whale's road, the gull's acres, brilliant,
    bonded and sound.

Jean

If you think it is easy to be in love, you have misheard.
Jean said yes to the war; she had a very Latin word
About coming back with your shield or on it, assumed with justice that I
would be undeterred,
Left me with an old red ring, a last kiss, and many letters I could reread
even when ever so slightly beer-slurred
In my sweltering troopship bound for shores where other loves were not to
be ignored.
        I hear her ringing laugh
        Cut through the draff and chaff
Like a knife-edge and after six decades I smile as I bend to burnish my
word-hoard.

War Voyage

A poet in a troopship – is it to the ends of the earth? – wake the anchor –
Hundreds of hammocks swaying and snoring – time for ribaldries, no
space for rancour –
Lashings of rain at first as we passed a ghostly rain-shrouded tanker –
South then, south round Africa, months of sweat, daily deck drills to make
us leaner and lanker –
Near Suez, admonitory slides in close-up of every kind and colour of
chancre –
        Water-watchers all
        Through sun and through squall
In case some sleekit dark sub from Kiel should pull an eerie flanker.

In Sidon

Cosgrove my closest companion that burning year on the Lebanese coast,
I have written about you already but raise you this last toast.
Nothing happened between us and that might seem a boast
Since there is pain in silence, but I never deserted the post
Of our vibrant daily intimacies even if the best and the worst
        Tore me for all to see
        Eyes down in decency.
So it was good, and I tell you this, I see you, your image is clear, you are in
my mind, you have not grown old, my Cosgrove, you are no ghost!

An Encounter 1

Those possible worlds that we see and cannot alter – oh they are a
      devastation!
The man beside me on the plane with his short-sleeved safari jacket
      needed no persuasion
To talk: we were friends, brothers, long before we reached the destination.
His wife on his other side was a mouse, never spoke: she was not part of an
      equation
That in word and look, hand on sleeve, pressed knee proved an instant
      mutual one-hour-long revelation
          Of impossible desire
          Which could only expire
As we took our separate ways on the tarmac, nursing elation, fighting
      desolation.

An Encounter 2

(In another universe, I poisoned her coffee and fled with Chuck to
      Amsterdam
Where we made some disguise and jumped onto a jangling tram
And snuggled into a brown café to smoke a little something and down the
      odd dram
And climbed to a steep high narrow room and lay there trying to cram
A lifetime into a night, pausing only to look down across the Dam
          And the dark canal
          Where even the banal
Quiver of a floating moon we took as a glory and in that universe, briefly,
      we were happy, without a qualm.)

Desire

It is a power, it is a mystery, it is a fate, but above all it is a power.
The jaws of Venus will not let go their prey. Hour after hour
They sink deeper, and the victim even smiles to see the spreading flower
Of blood, as it springs from those scary threshings of life. Don't cower,
Don't wince! It's only a nightmare, it's only a movie, it's only imaginary
     Phaedra shrieking from her tower.
            'Only, only' you cry?
            What do you want to deny?
Are you trying to tell us all these flecks of blood are not from something
     struggling to be born? You think it's like the passing sting of some
     damned April shower?

Love

Love rules. Love laughs. Love marches. Love is the wolf that guards the
     gate.
Love is the food of music, art, poetry. It fills us and fuels us and fires us to
     create.
Love is terror. Love is sweat. Love is bashed pillow, crumpled sheet,
     unenviable fate.
Love is the honour that kills and saves and nothing will ever let that high
     ambiguity abate.
Love is the crushed ice that tingles and shivers and clinks fidgin-fain for
     the sugar-drenched absinth to fall on it and alter its state.
            With love you send a probe
            So far from the globe
No one can name the shoals the voids the belts the zones the drags the
     flares it signals all to leave all and to navigate.

After a Lecture

Last and most unexpected friend, do you know you overthrew me
In those first moments when you walked towards me in that lecture-room,
  not to undo me
But you did undo me, I was shaking, I felt that well-known spear go
  through me,
And when we talked my mind was racing like a computer to keep that
  contact sparking. What drew me
Was irreducible but recognisable– drythroat fragments, physical
  certainties, emanations and invasions so quick to imbue me
      And wound me with hope
      I swore I would cope
With whatever late late lifeline this man, whom I knew I loved, picked up
  and threw me.

Plans

Mark, here we are, here we go, let us celebrate four years of letters and talk,
Purdey and Dostoevsky and Glenmorangie and a splash of Pasolini will
  never be out of stock
I assure you, and although when you are in Italy it is true I may watch the
  clock
For your safe return, there is nothing north or south that is able to block
Our invisible communication. With it we shall live to unlock
      Something quite sizable
      Perhaps inadvisable! –
Oh I don't know what, leave it for the shock, we don't want anything to
  scatter off at half-cock.

Brickies

Scaffolding rises like a forest round the six storeys of Whittingehame Court.
The metal poles are hammered into place, the planks are laid, the brickies
    are at their sport
Of scampering up the near-vertical ladders, our fort
Bristles with a bantering excrescence of life which is, well, art of a sort.
'For a full picture,' you said, 'for the full Brueghel we need female brickies
    in skirts – short!'
        'They'd have jeans,' I said,
        So keep a cool head.'
'Use your imagination, man. That hoot from the Clyde! It's a boatload of
    feisty busty brickies getting their black-leather-skirted arse into port!'

Italy

You'll be in Florence now, my man, and is there scaffolding on the *duomo*,
    or only history and the sun?
Ghostly Etruscan backchat even before the city was begun?
A whiff of Savonarola? Or are pigeons with cameras the new smoking gun
To show that tourism rules, obliterates, takes a story that will run and run
And runs with it, high art, dropping a dim litter of Goth and Hun?
        Tell me when you come back.
        I'm peering through a crack
In the dusty polythene at distant Italy, and you, where you may be, what
    you will do, what you have done.

Whistling

What a blessing it is when you have memories that sustain you
Through absence and distance that otherwise would drain you
Of hope and therefore of will! Love will never not pain you
But at the end of pain there is someone who will not disdain you
And a slipstream of joy from Glasgow to Firenze can hardly contain you
        As you break the clouds
        To jostle the crowds
Where Mark might be whistling a snatch or a catch that would carelessly
    care for you and sain you.

Harry

– Tell us about Harry. – Harry the vanman? – The very man. Go ahead.
– Where shall I begin? He delivered newspapers and the van was red.
– That's not too interesting. – We used to play strip draughts before we
    went to bed.
We lit out for the Blackpool Illuminations instead of trolling the Med.
I am sure there are many other things that might be said.
        – So he's not a fixture.
        I get the picture.
– Do you? I don't think so. Wayward paths can be affectionately led.

The Last Dragon

Is it the mists of autumn? My mind's dislodged, far back, far off, in
    turmoil, a memory trail
To the grizzled warrior in Heorot hall whose heart *inne weoll*
Thonne he wintrum frod worn gemunde and told his ancient tale.
I too am old in winters and stories and may I never fail
To guard my word-hoard before the dragon with his flailing tail
        Sweeps everything away
        Leaves nothing to say
Either in turmoil or in peace, and neither poetry nor song nor all their
    longing can avail.

Dragon on Watch

My grandmother's bronze dragon straddles my mantelpiece like a guard,
Heavy, fierce, Chinese, and now quite old, he shows no sign of not being
    hard
If activated. I have just been dusting his tongue which licks out like a
    flame. Fine, unmarred,
His ears and horns are flames, his tail is flames, his arched reptilian back is
    unscarred.
He will certainly outlive me, but to eat me – that's barred!
        He can watch over Mark
        When I am in the dark.
Polish him with respect, with a dry cloth, and the house will never be
    ill-starred.

Scan Day

Two scans in one day, CT and bone – they are certainly looking after me.
Computerised tomography like a non-invasive Vesalius will slice me apart
    to see
If I am really what I ought to be and not what I don't want to be.
In the giant redwood forest you are shown the rings of a fallen tree
With the few blips and wavy bits that tell you it's been a good fight, even
    with destiny.
        There are no chimeras
        Under the cameras.
You are laid out as you are, imperfect, waiting, wondering, approximately
    free.

Skeleton Day

Bizarrely brought, demanding thought, the benedictions of the bone scan!
There you lie, well-injected, clothed but motionless man
As the machine lowers its load close over you and begins its creeping pan
Downwards, while the screen unrolls a little skeleton, a blueprint, a plan –
That plan is you! Skull, ribs, hips emerge from the dark like a caravan
        Bound for who knows where
        Stepping through earth or air
Still of a piece and still en route, beating out the music of tongs and bones
    while it can.

October Day

Get the sun out, get it shining! It's only October, and only a tenth of the
    leaves are yellowing.
Prod a few white clouds out of their beds and get them billowing!
We can sit a while and not batten down the hatches for a gale following.
We can clink a glass and swirl the wine and still not rush the swallowing.
We can smoke in a moveless dear afternoon till the late light spreads its
    hallowing
        Over everything
        And then we must bring
The day to rest with good ease, recollections, far thoughts, love and
    dallying.

Titania

Scratch him between the ears, he is in excellent fettle, and when he listens
    to the tongs and bones
He nods his head, brays gently in time, and his hurdy-gurdy drones
Ravish Titania who has fled from pavanes and protocols trumpets and
    thrones
To be with her beast, to cuddle her cuddy, to dawdle with her donkey, to
    translate his tones
Into transports of love. So why is it touching? You don't need erogenous
    zones
        For a parable of affection
        Doomed in direction
But groping for the gold that's panned from gainless pains and groans.

Tatyana

Tatyana sat at her little window table in the moonlight.
First love forbade her even to ask whether it was wise to write.
Her nightgown slipped from her shoulder as she made her heart naked all
    that long night.
Her letter fell dead. Onegin thought her naive, provincial, and not very
    bright.
Bright enough to marry money, but glittering at a ball, poised and mature
    in the candlelight,
        She knew that happiness
        Was really something else,
Was once *tak vozmozhno, tak blizko*, so possible, so near, and now only
    remembered, receded, almost out of sight.

Teresa

Up here in Ávila, and grand the sierra, there's so much air and space for
    vision.
God must be nearer by a sky or two. It burns. He burns. And there is no
    remission.
There's love, and love, and then there's love – and love – and if you are
    really aflame, who makes the decision?
I'm a bustler, I'm a hustler, I'm a hussy, I have a mission, I make an
    incision, I court collision.
Who do I love? My barefoot sisters, Juan de la Cruz who might be my son,
    the intuition
        I have of one divine
        Lover who will be mine
But not till I die. Ah, *muero porque no muero!* God forgive my ardent
    impatient admission!

John 1

Nothing will bring him back. I know that, of course I know that. The days
When I do not think of him are few, but if I turn my gaze
On a phantom, on a plot of earth, on a faded photograph of great times, I
    raise
Nothing, nearly nothing, no, not nothing, it is the something of a pain that
    stays
Ineradicable and only to be mitigated when I breathe the phrase
        I loved you. You must know
        It was truly so, although
As clay in clay you cannot catch my thanks, my steadiness, my lateness,
    my praise.

Once you dyed your greying hair with a black marker and the pillow was a
    mess.
What did I care? What did you care? We were in such happiness
It might have been peach pink or saltire blue. And as for dress
My flares were wider than yours – oh no they weren't – oh yes they were –
    confess!
Faffing along the scorching Black Sea coast we were burnt too raw to
    caress.
            At Constantsa we were blest
            By a breeze from the west
Unforgiving Ovid stared down at us, but even in that half-decayed port we
    could not share a smidgen of his distress.

When in Thrace

Ovid had to start wearing furs – layers of them sometimes – in Thrace.
He said the winter winds and the salt sleet would cut off your face.
He threeped and threeped that his exile was a conspiracy and a disgrace.
Surrealistic metamorphoses of love and lust were hardly to be written
    about in that place.
But once he learned to stop girning and moaning he uncovered a trace
            Of common humanity
            Cast off urbanity
Wrote poems in the barbarian tongue which he hated but which was now,
    as a philosopher would one day say, the case.

Lust

Lust is a languorous pot of fumes in the hallway. Lust is steam-pistons.
    Lust is promises promises.
Lust is a bead-curtain chinkled by a dancer's nipples as she shakes and
    shines through the teasing interstices.
Lust rides the wildebeest into oblivion. On its back are princes, blisters,
    mistresses.
Lust is the corer screwing and sloshing its juicy cock-shaped tunnel into
    the melon of your wishes.
Lust is the holding of a sweaty glance across the gay disco's heaving
    dance-floor and its bareback vistas.
        It is really not very good
        And we don't think you should
But we know you will. Dinners come brimming from the kitchen and you
    grin as you crunch the ashes from those hot hot dishes.

Late Day

There are days when, and there are days if, and then again there are
    simply days.
After a long night, after a bad night, the sun did let out a few rays
That filtered gamely through the grimy scaffolding. The poor wintry stuff
    gets my praise.
If darkness kept the world like a closed eye, we could only get our
    nightmare to search and gaze
From its rolling red and bridled eyeball as we ride it down and down
    where muzzles never graze.
        How great the winter sun
        When horrors are undone
By gentlest flimsiest fingers lighting our fingers as we open the curtains on
    a day content to glimmer and not to blaze.

Bobby

Bobby on one elbow, stretched out in his red jeans on my carpet, thirty
years ago
Bobby at the Grand Canyon, squinting up, on the verge, fathomless
purple below
Bobby a bundle of nerves as the transatlantic plane comes down to land,
heavy and slow
Bobby mugged, compensated, an unexpected few thousands to blow
Bobby with a stick and a cap and a fluttery heart in a basement café in our
Glasgow
Where we faithfully meet
Take the lift to the street
Having swirled out our foamy chocolate-sprinkled late but oh not last
cappuccino!

G.

'Ah canny say Ah love ye but.' 'I know, that's all right, it's all right.'
'Ah love ma wife an ma weans. Ah don't go aroon thinkin aboot you day an
night.
Ah wahnt tae come in yir mooth, an see thee teeth a yours – see they don't
bite!
Ah like ye right enough, but aw that lovey-dovey stuff is pure shite.
Ah widny kiss ye, God no.' But kiss me he did one afternoon, with a drink
in him, at Central Station, on the lips, in broad daylight.
It will not be denied
In this life. It is a flood-tide
You may dam with all your language but it breaks and bullers through and
blatters all platitudes and protestations before it, clean out of sight.

Tomtits

Two twinkling tomtits were enjoying the scaffolding outside my window.
    Did they think it was a tree?
Surely they are not going to nest in those hard angles for all the world to
    see?
Against the filthy struts the sodden planks the louring sky they are new-
    minted fresh and free,
Flashing flirting blue and yellow, dark eyes darting missing nothing, not
    even me! –
A pair, an item, a unit, so magnetic to each other and so beautiful to us
    that we say they must be
          In love, what else could wind
          The springs of heart and mind
To frisk through all that muck and murk in such precarious liberty?

Arabian Night

The runners through the darkness hear the hooves, is it behind them or all
    round?
They are inured to the unknown and only wonder idly at the sound.
They track the stony desert to bring back the bride, all braided and bound
With silver and leather, silent, white-veiled and white-gowned.
Why did one of them not hunker down and set his ear to the ground?
          Jealous riders jumped them
          Sabred them and dumped them
But the bright bride had learned to hide, stripped off her braws, put on
    her shades, called her maids, packed a van and roared off, never to be
    found.

November Night

Dark and darker the year, late leaves flying, my thoughts turning
Back to '38, war looming, lectures distracting, feelings racing, engrossing,
    burning,
Jean and Frank together within me smouldering shouldering laughing
    tugging churning,
Frank the first, king of something, emerging, emulating, energising, a
    whole province of yearning,
Gallus Russianist, stocky communist, quick-talking anti-somnambulist,
    your learning
        Was my learning, but then
        You were the first of men
In that impossible dimension of love which now with unspoken groans and
    even secret tears I was approaching and discerning.

Spanish Night

And yet, *en una noche oscura*, as we know from the words of swarthy much-
    buffeted John of the Cross,
In the darkest night, from a dungeon, a real one, rich in hideous shit and
    chains and slime and moss,
It is not impossible to bribe a jailer and bamboozle his guttering god like a
    joss,
Escaping from dark into dark but leaving great doctors to gloss
What light he saw then in the stars he sent his thankful, his hot, his loving
    thoughts across.
        He sank onto the breast
        Of one whom he loved best
Delirious among the dim night lilies where at last there was neither loved
    nor lover, but there was love and everything that was not love was
    dross.

Whatever Happened To

the young man sitting next to me in the Biograph (peace to its long-lost
    rubble!), in that smoky place
Where it was too dark to take stock of anybody's face,
Who seized my wandering hand, laid it flat palm upwards, and with his
    index finger started to trace
I.L.O.V.E.Y.O.U., clear as if he had spoken, letter by steady letter,
    crossing with quick grace
My life-line and my heart-line and moving into a space
        He was not blate to invade
        But was he then afraid
Scurrying off as if in shame that he had laid the train for some outrageous
    embrace?

Absence

Love is the most mysterious of the winds that blow.
As you lie alone it batters with sleeplessness at the winter bedroom window.
The friend is absent, the streetlamp shivers desolately to and fro.
Your prostate makes you get up, you look out, police car and ambulance
    howl and flash as they matter-of-factly come and go.
There is pain and danger down there, greater than the pain you know
        But it is pain all the same
        As you breathe the absent name
Of one who is bonded to you beyond blizzards, time-zones, sickness, black
    stars, snow.

Letters

You sent a card from the Uffizi which took sixteen days to reach these
    shores.
A pigeon might be better, it could home in on the scaffold and count the
    floors.
The heart beats, I sit, I eat, I talk, I open doors
But in the everyday I am waiting for the imagined but stormily cargoed
    shores
Of joy and hope a letter in your upright hand tips out and restores.
        'Scrivimi!' you write.
        I do, I will, all right!
But this, though I do not send it, I give you to keep till the sun melts the
    rocks and the sea no longer roars.

Love and the Worlds

Scary is this tremulous earth, flaring, shouting, killing and being killed.
Is the universe rippling with life? What sign is there that space is filled
With anything but gas and dust and fire and rock? Are we the tillers to
    have it tilled?
I think so! And with these red hands, an act of love? Why not? We cry but
    we create, we kill but we build.
Dante was sure the stars were all – even ours – rolled out by love. They gild
        A dark that would truly scare
        If there was nothing there
The horror of there not being something, good or bad or neither, made or
    found, willed or self-willed.

The Release

The scaffolding has gone. The sky is there! hard cold high clear and blue.
Clanking poles and thudding planks were the music of a strip-down that
    let light through
At last, hammered the cage door off its hinges, banged its goodbye to the
    bantering dusty brickie crew,
Left us this rosy cliff-face telling the tentative sun it is almost as good as
    new.
So now that we are so scoured and open and clean, what shall we do?
        There is so much to say
        And who can delay
When some are lost and some are seen, our dearest heads, and to those and
    to these we must still answer and be true.

September–November 2002

The War on the War on Terror

This woman, I heard her say she could not bear
To bring a child into a world so dreadful
It scoops up smoking body parts *like that.*
Did she mean she would rather leave them lying?
Of course not, that's just twisting what she says.
Well, let's be blunt, let us be damnably blunt.
Would you rather not have a baby in a body-bag,
Are you listening? – bits of a baby
In a body-bag, would you rather not have that,
Not see that, not touch that, not know that,
Is it too much for you, for your sensibilities,
Come on, I know what I am talking about,
I have been right through life like an arrow.
What child would welcome such a grudging mother?
Stay in bed then; count the hours and wars.
It really is a very simple question:
Would you rather have something, or nothing?
Sit with your back against some tomb, altar,
Observatory if that's what it is, Callanish
Will do, and empty your mind of everything
But Callanish, and then give Callanish
The kick, it takes at least a day and a night
For strongest ancient markers to dissolve
With all their people, artefacts, lastly all power
If you believe me, as I think you should –
And there is no word for what is left –
Imagine an eternity of this –
You, childless woman who wants to remain so,
You are frowning in this tawdry restaurant
And I do not know your beliefs, if any,
But I outstare you with my unspoken thought
That the greatest gift it is possible to make
Is life itself.
                    Gather your things, off
Into the grimy evening,
Woman unknown, best so.

Conversation in Palestine

– Your learned friends have been asking about you.
  Where have you been and what have you seen?
– I walk round the lake and I collect people.
– That is not what I would call promising.
– Nothing not based on the ordinary will ever succeed.
– A face floating past the jamb of the door:
  is that ordinary? People talk.
– My mother, with a candle! She doesn't sleep.
  Find better evidence than that. She's ordinary.
  I'm ordinary. I go to the temple,
  ask some very simple questions. They bridle,
  they splutter, they say respect your elders.
  Well, there's another who's even younger,
  not being born yet, but once my Wittgenstein
  gets the bit between his teeth, oho,
  or shall we say a simple ordinary poker,
  they might complain indeed: give him a chance
  he'll change the world, give me a chance I'll change
  the world, and while I'm at it there's my mother
  who has already changed the world in having me,
  an ordinary man in Galilee.
– What is so great about this Winterheim?
– Wittgenstein.
                    Whatever. What has he done,
  or rather, what will he do, if I believe you?
– Give away a fortune. Don't you like that?
  Ferociously honest, a life pared to the bone.
  If you want processions, hierarchies,
  he's not your man. Swish vestments
  are anathema to my father
  I can tell you that, and to me too
  if it comes to it, and I go further:
  white robes disingenuously simple
  are worse than any magisterium's twinkle.
  Stand under the poplars in the park
  says Wittgenstein, and it will come to you.
– What will?
                I have said.
                            The stars will soon be out.
– I think so: the beam, the blinter, and the blaze.